Hamlyn
low-fat
Cooking

Hamlyn
low-fat
Cooking

Over 120 recipes, with 5g of fat or less

First published in 1998 by Hamlyn
an imprint of Octopus Publishing Group Ltd
Michelin House, 81 Fulham Road, London SW3 6RB

Copyright © 1999 Octopus Publishing Group Ltd

Printed in China

Publishing Director: Laura Bamford

Commissioning Editor: Nicky Hill
Assistant Editor: Cara Frost

Creative Director: Keith Martin
Senior Designer: Geoff Fennell

Indexer: Pamela Le Gassick
Nutritional analyst: Carol Bateman

Senior Production Controller: Joanna Walker

NOTES

- All the recipes in this book have been analysed by a professional nutritionist, so that you can see their nutritional content at a glance. The abbreviations are as follows:
  Kcal = calories
  KJ = kilojoules
  CHO = carbohydrate.
  The analysis refers to each portion

- Both metric and imperial measurements have been given in all recipes. Use one set of measurements only and not a mixture of both.

- Standard level spoon measurements are used in all recipes.
  1 tablespoon = one 15 ml spoon
  1 teaspoon = one 5 ml spoon

- Eggs should be medium to large unless otherwise stated.

- Milk should be skimmed unless otherwise stated.

- Meat and poultry should be cooked thoroughly. To test if poultry is cooked, pierce the flesh through the thickest part with a skewer or fork – the juices should run clear, never pink or red. Do not re-freeze poultry that has been frozen previously and thawed.

- Do not re-freeze a dish that has been frozen previously.

- Pepper should be freshly ground black pepper unless otherwise stated.

- Fresh herbs should be used, unless otherwise stated. If unavailable, use dried herbs as an alternative but halve the quantities stated.

- Measurements for canned food have been given as a standard metric equivalent.

- Ovens should be preheated to the specified temperature – if using a fan-assisted oven, follow the manufacturer's instructions for adjusting the time and the temperature.

Contents

Introduction

On a daily basis it is wise to keep clear of highly fatty foods and increase your intake of foods high in protein and carbohydrates. Fats are high in calories and can contribute to some extent to weight problems. The incidence of coronary heart disease has increased dramatically in the past 50 years or so, and medical research has identified several major causes. One of these is too high a consumption of saturated fats which may cause raised blood cholesterol; meat and dairy products are the worst offenders, but the consumption of these can be reduced and there are many other delicious foods that can be eaten in their place. We aim to show you here that this doesn't necessarily mean missing out on flavour or compromising on nutrition, it just means adopting a slightly different approach to choosing and using foods – selecting healthy ingredients, using herbs, spices and flavourings to add flavour and not fat, and marinating food before cooking in wine, herbs, spices and garlic.

Fat

Fat adds moisture to food so it is essential that when cooking without it, the food doesn't dry out. This can be done by covering with foil, or basting with stock or water so that the food almost steams and the natural flavours come through. Herbs and spices can also be used to add flavour without adding fat.

Oils – olive oil and rapeseed oil are high in monounsaturated fats, which may help to protect against heart disease. In addition, rapeseed oil is high in vitamin E.

Spray oils – these are excellent when frying as it is easier to use less oil than from a bottle. Look for extra virgin olive oil spray.

Low-fat spreads – these contain a high proportion of water and are not suitable for cooking but they are an excellent substitute to margarine and butter for reducing calories and total fat intake. Do check the fat content on the packaging.

Dairy Produce

Dairy products such as milk, butter, cream, cheese and ice cream are one of the main sources of saturated fats. Sometimes all that is needed is to replace the usual products that you buy with low-fat alternatives.

Skimmed milk – this is fresh cows' milk with a fat content of no more than 0.3% (often 0.1%). This milk is therefore ideal for anyone wishing to cut down on their fat intake. It is not suitable for babies and children as the fat soluble vitamins A and D are removed with the fat, although other nutrient levels remain the same. The milk looks thin and can be used in tea and coffee as well as in soups, sauces and cakes.

Semi-skimmed milk – this has a fat content of 1.5–1.8% and tastes less rich than full-cream milk.

Smatana – this is a soured cream made from skimmed milk, single cream and a souring culture, making it a good low-fat substitute for cream. It should be added towards the end of the cooking time and not allowed to boil as it will curdle.

Crème fraîche – this is a cream that has been treated with a culture that gives it a light acidity without sourness. It is an important ingredient in French cooking. Use low-fat crème fraîche wherever possible.

Low-fat yogurt – made from concentrated skimmed milk, this has between 0.5 and 2% fat. If possible use very low fat yogurt which contains less than 0.5% fat.

Full-fat soft cheese – this is lower in fat than cream cheese, both are unripened cows' milk cheese made from cream. It is soft and white with a smooth texture. It is often used to make cheesecakes.

Cottage cheese – this is a white, granular cheese with a clean, mild taste. It is available plain or flavoured with herbs, fruit or vegetables. It is also available in low-fat varieties. Cottage cheese is a type of curd cheese made from skimmed cows' milk.

Virtually fat-free fromage frais – this is fresh curd cheese made from pasteurized skimmed cows' milk. Its consistency varies from soft, light and pourable to relatively thick and firm. The flavour is mildly acidic and the fat content is almost nil.

Cream substitutes – there are a number of cream substitutes on the market made from vegetable fats and water. These are lower in fat than real cream but have an inferior taste.

Light mozzarella – mozzarella is an unripened cheese from Italy which was originally made from buffaloes' milk. Nowadays cows' milk is more commonly used. Mozzarella is white and spongy with a mild, creamy-sour taste and is traditionally shaped into balls. The low-fat variety is often labelled 'light'.

Low-fat cheeses – some cheeses such as Cheddar and Cheshire can be bought labelled 'reduced fat'. These are made in a similar way to traditional hard cheeses but with about half the fat content; low-fat cheeses tend to have a milder flavour than full-fat cheeses.

Quark – a fresh curd cheese made throughout Germany from cows' milk. The variety made with skimmed milk contains the least fat. Quark is white, with a spoonable texture and delicate sour taste.

Edam – this is a semi-hard cheese from Holland which is well known for its red wax coat and ball shape. It is made from pasteurized skimmed cows' milk and is low in calories. Edam is golden yellow with a supple texture, a sparse scattering of holes and a nutty taste.

Meat

Try to limit portions of red meat to 75 g/3 oz and choose the leanest cuts possible whenever you can. Remove all traces of visible fat before cooking the meat. If mince is required, it is better to buy very lean cuts of steak, such as sirloin, and mince it yourself or get your butcher to do this for you. If you buy prepacked mince it is difficult to tell how much fat there actually is. When roasting meat, always place a rack in the bottom of the roasting tin so that the meat does not actually sit in its own juices. Grilling and griddling are much healthier methods of cooking meat than frying as no extra fat is needed.

Poultry and game – such as rabbit, venison, pigeon, partridge and pheasant, are nearly always a lot lower in fat than red meat and contain more polyunsaturated fat and less saturated fat than other meats. Chicken and turkey are a lot leaner than goose and duck, though the fat is less saturated than in red meats. Most of the fat in poultry is found just beneath the skin, so it is advisable always to use lean parts of the bird, such as the breast, and to remove the skin and trim away any visible fat.

Fish and Shellfish

Fish is an excellent source of protein and very low in fat. White fish such as cod, coley, haddock, whiting and skate are low in fat. Fatty fish, such as mackerel, herring, sardines, tuna, salmon and trout are all excellent sources of polyunsaturated oils. If using canned fish, such as tuna, sardines and salmon, choose ones that have been preserved in brine or spring water rather than oil. Steaming, poaching and microwaving are all excellent methods of cooking fresh fish without the addition of fat. Steaming or baking fish in parcels of greaseproof paper or foil with herbs and flavourings is an ideal method of cooking as it seals in all the flavour. Many shellfish including prawns, lobster and crab are very low in fat although prawns actually contain a higher level of cholesterol, weight for weight, than meat and poultry.

Fruits, Vegetables and Grains

Fruit provides a ready source of energy because it is rich in natural sugar (fructose), and minerals and vitamins are present in most fruit. Fruit is also a good source of dietary fibre and low in calories. Choose from fruit is season such as apples, bananas, strawberries, raspberries, apricots, cherries, currants, grapes and kiwi fruit. Vegetables are very important to a balanced diet. They provide minerals, vitamins and fibre and some such as potatoes and parsnips provide carbohydrate. Some vegetables such as pulses provide protein, but most vegetables are low in protein and low in fat. Olives and avocados are the exception as they are both high in fat. There are an enormous variety of exotic vegetables and salads available and they can be prepared in innumerable ways. Pulses are rich in protein, carbohydrate and vitamins and minerals. They are also inexpensive and extremely versatile. Fresh pasta contains eggs which adds extra fat so for a low-fat diet use dried pasta which just contains durum wheat and water. Wholewheat pasta is healthier as it contains the whole wheat grain, which provides more protein and fibre. Rice supplies many important nutrients and minerals such as potassium and phosphorus.

Nuts and Seeds

These are high in fat and calories. They are cholesterol free and their fat is unsaturated.

Foods to avoid

Highly processed foods such as crisps and snacks, biscuits and cakes, tend to contain a lot of fat and so do processed meats, sausages and mayonnaise. As a rule fresh fruit and vegetables and freshly prepared foods are the best choice.

Low-fat Cooking Techniques

Poaching, steaming, baking in foil, stir-frying, microwaving, grilling, griddling and barbecuing are all excellent low-fat cooking methods, rather than deep- and shallow-frying and roasting. It is a good idea to use non-stick saucepans and woks so less fat is needed.

Homemade Stocks

Nothing beats the flavour of homemade stock if you have the time. Also by making your own, you can monitor your fat intake more accurately. The following are high flavour but low fat stocks:

Vegetable Stock

3 potatoes, chopped

1 onion, sliced

2 leeks, chopped

2 celery sticks, chopped

2 carrots, chopped

1 small fennel head, thinly sliced

few sprigs of thyme

few parsley stalks

2 bay leaves

salt and pepper

1 Put all the vegetables into a saucepan with the herbs and 1.5 litres/2½ pints water. Bring to the boil slowly, then skim.

2 Add salt and pepper to taste. Simmer, covered, for about 1½ hours. Skim the stock 3–4 times during cooking.

3 Strain the stock through clean muslin or a very fine sieve. Cool quickly and store in the refrigerator until required.

Makes about 1 litre/1¾ pints

Fish Stock

1 kg/2 lb fish trimmings

1 small onion, finely chopped

2 leeks, chopped

1 bay leaf

few parsley stalks

few sprigs of fennel

large piece of lemon rind

200 ml/7 fl oz dry white wine

salt and pepper

1 Place the fish trimmings in a large saucepan with the onion, leeks, bay leaf, parsley, fennel, lemon rind and 1.5 litres/2½ pints water. Slowly bring to the boil, then skim any surface scum.

2 Add the white wine, and salt and pepper to taste and simmer very gently for 30 minutes, skimming the stock once or twice during cooking.

3 Strain the stock through clean muslin or a very fine sieve. Cool quickly and store in the refrigerator until required.

Makes about 1 litre/1¾ pints

Chicken Stock

1 chicken carcass, plus giblets

1 onion, chopped

2 large carrots, chopped

1 celery stick, chopped

1 bay leaf

few parsley stalks

1 thyme sprig

salt and pepper

1 Remove any skin or fat from the chicken carcass and chop into small pieces. Place in a large saucepan with the giblets, onions, carrots, celery, bay leaf, parsley stalks, thyme and 1.8 litres/3 pints of water.

2 Bring to the boil and skim, removing any scum or fat that remains on the surface. Lower the heat and simmer for 2–2½ hours, skimming the stock once or twice during cooking.

3 Strain the stock through clean muslin or a very fine sieve. Cool quickly and store in the refrigerator until required.

Makes about 1 litre/1¾ pints

soups and

These simple, eye-catching soups and starters include refreshing chilled soups. The chunkier soups could be served with bread to make a satisfying, healthy lunch.

starters

yellow pepper
soup

Serves	**5**
Preparation time	**15–20** minutes
Cooking time	**50–55** minutes
Kcal	**100**
KJ	**425**
Protein	**2** g
Fat	**5** g
CHO	**11** g

3 yellow peppers, cored and
    deseeded
50 g/2 oz butter or margarine
1 small onion, chopped
1.2 litres/2 pints Vegetable Stock
    (see page 11)
1 teaspoon mild curry powder
¼ teaspoon turmeric
1 tablespoon chopped fresh
    coriander, or 1 teaspoon dried
    leaf coriander
300 g/10 oz potatoes, peeled and
    chopped
salt

1 Chop one pepper finely and place it in a small saucepan, then chop the remaining peppers roughly.

2 Melt 25 g/1 oz of the butter or margarine in another saucepan and cook the onion and roughly chopped peppers for 5 minutes, stirring frequently. Stir in the stock, curry powder, turmeric and coriander, season with salt, then add the potatoes. Bring to the boil, then lower the heat and simmer, partially covered, for 40–45 minutes, or until the vegetables are very soft.

3 Melt the remaining butter with the finely chopped pepper in the small pan. Cook over a gentle heat until the pepper is very soft. Reserve for the garnish.

4 Purée the onion, pepper and potato mixture in batches in a blender or food processor until very smooth. Return to a clean saucepan and reheat gently, taste and adjust the seasoning if necessary. Serve in warmed soup plates or bowls, garnished with a little of the sautéed chopped yellow pepper.

Sweet yellow peppers are milder in flavour than green ones. All peppers are rich in vitamin C.

orange
consommé

6	Serves
5 minutes, plus chilling	Preparation time
5 minutes	Cooking time
35	Kcal
150	KJ
3 g	Protein
0 g	Fat
6 g	CHO

1 Pour the consommé into a pan. Add the orange juice to the pan with the cloves and cayenne to taste. Bring the mixture to the boil, then remove the cloves, using a slotted spoon. Tip the contents of the pan into a bowl and set aside until cool.

475 g/15 oz can beef consommé
juice of 3 oranges
2 cloves
cayenne pepper (optional)
1 orange, thinly sliced, to garnish

2 When the orange consommé is cool, cover the surface closely and chill for 3–4 hours in the refrigerator. Alternatively freeze the mixture for about 30 minutes, until the surface is covered with a thin layer of ice.

3 Serve the orange consommé in chilled bowls, garnishing each serving with an orange slice, if liked.

A deliciously refreshing starter to any meal. The preparation takes hardly any time at all and, if you want to speed up the chilling process, cool and cover the consommé, then place it in the freezer until the surface is covered with a thin layer of ice.

chilled watercress

soup

Serves	**8**
Preparation time	about **10** minutes, plus chilling
Cooking time	**25** minutes
Kcal	**60**
KJ	**246**
Protein	**3** g
Fat	**2** g
CHO	**9** g

1 tablespoon oil

1 onion, chopped

2 bunches of watercress, thick stems discarded, coarsely chopped

1 tablespoon flour

750 ml/1¼ pints Vegetable Stock (see page 11)

1 potato, cut into 1 cm/½ inch dice

pinch of grated nutmeg

2 heaped tablespoons dried skimmed milk powder

salt and pepper

to garnish (optional):

a few watercress leaves

1 tablespoon olive oil

1 Heat the oil in a saucepan. Add the onion and watercress and cook over a moderate heat for 10 minutes, stirring frequently. Remove from the heat and stir in the flour. Return to the heat, stirring until thickened. Add the stock, potatoes and nutmeg, and salt and pepper to taste, bring to the boil, then lower the heat and simmer, covered, for 15–20 minutes, or until the potatoes are soft. Leave to cool slightly.

2 Purée the mixture in batches in a food processor or blender. Transfer to a large bowl, cover closely and chill in the refrigerator for at least 3 hours.

3 Just before serving, add the dried milk and blend until smooth. Taste and adjust the seasoning. Serve in chilled bowls, garnishing each portion with a few watercress leaves and a little olive oil, if using, and black pepper.

Watercress is pleasantly pungent and gives an almost peppery flavour to this cold soup.

spinach soup

25 g/1 oz butter or margarine

1 onion, chopped

250 g/8 oz fresh or frozen spinach,
   thawed if frozen

600 ml/1 pint Vegetable Stock (see
   page 11)

1 potato, thinly sliced

1 teaspoon lemon juice

pinch of grated nutmeg

100 ml/3½ fl oz semi-skimmed milk

salt and white pepper

ground almonds, to garnish
   (optional)

1 Heat the butter or margarine in a heavy-based saucepan. Add the onion and cook over a moderate heat until soft but not golden. Add the spinach and cook until soft, stirring constantly.

2 Pour the stock into the pan and add the potato, lemon juice and nutmeg. Season with salt and pepper to taste. Cook, partially covered, over a moderate heat for 10–12 minutes, or until the potato is soft.

3 Purée the mixture in a food processor or blender until smooth. Return to a clean saucepan. Add the milk and heat the soup gently without boiling. Transfer to heated soup bowls, sprinkling each portion with ground almonds, to garnish, if liked.

Although frozen leaf spinach can be used for this recipe, the full-flavoured taste of fresh spinach cannot be matched.

pea and mint
soup

Serves	**6**
Preparation time	**5–10** minutes
Cooking time	**30–35** minutes
Kcal	**148**
KJ	**624**
Protein	**7** g
Fat	**5** g
CHO	**20** g

25 g/1 oz butter or margarine

1 small onion, chopped

500 g/1 lb frozen green peas

¼ teaspoon sugar

1.2 litres/2 pints Chicken or
  Vegetable Stock (see page 11)

4 tablespoons chopped mint

300 g/10 oz potatoes, peeled and
  coarsely chopped

150 ml/¼ pint semi-skimmed milk

salt and white pepper

1 Melt the butter or margarine in a saucepan, add the onion and cook over a moderate heat until soft but not golden, stirring frequently.

2 Add the peas, sugar, stock and 3 tablespoons of the chopped mint. Stir in white pepper to taste and bring the mixture to the boil. Add the potatoes, lower the heat and simmer, partially covered, for 20–25 minutes.

3 Purée the mixture in batches in a food processor or blender until smooth. Return to a clean saucepan, season with salt, add the milk and stir well. Heat the soup gently without boiling. Serve in warmed soup plates or bowls, garnished with the remaining chopped mint.

To serve chilled, transfer the soup to a bowl after puréeing. Add the milk and season with salt. Allow the soup to cool, then cover closely and chill for at least 3 hours. Serve in chilled bowls, garnished with mint.

parsnip
and carrot soup

4 Serves

15 minutes Preparation time

about **30** minutes Cooking time

70 Kcal

298 KJ

3 g Protein

1 g Fat

14 g CHO

250 g/8 oz parsnips, chopped

250 g/8 oz carrots, chopped

1 onion, chopped

600 ml/1 pint Chicken Stock (see
   page 11)

salt and pepper

natural yogurt, to garnish

1 Place the parsnips, carrots and onion in a large saucepan with the stock and season with salt and pepper. Bring to the boil, cover and simmer for 20 minutes, or until the vegetables are tender.

2 Remove from the heat and allow to cool slightly, then purée in a food processor or blender until smooth, or press through a fine sieve.

3 Return the soup to the cleaned pan and reheat. Serve hot in individual warmed soup bowls, garnished with yogurt.

The humble, inexpensive parsnip can be transformed into a number of delicious soups.

carrot and sage
soup

Serves	**6**
Preparation time	**15** minutes
Cooking time	about **1** hour
Kcal	**87**
KJ	**360**
Protein	**2** g
Fat	**4** g
CHO	**0** g

25 g/1 oz butter

1 large onion, finely chopped

750 g/1½ lb carrots, finely sliced

900 ml/1½ pints Vegetable Stock
   (see page 11)

1 tablespoon chopped sage

salt and pepper

sage sprigs, to garnish (optional)

1 Melt the butter in a large heavy-based pan, add the onion and gently fry until soft but not golden, then add the carrots and stock. Season with salt and pepper.

2 Bring to the boil and simmer uncovered for about 30 minutes.

3 Purée the soup in a food processor or blender until smooth, then return to a clean pan and add the chopped sage. Bring to the boil and simmer for another 15 minutes.

4 Serve in warmed soup bowls or plates, garnished with sage sprigs, if liked.

Fresh sage is often unavailable during the winter months, but dried sage may be used instead. Soak it first in a tablespoon of warmed white wine.

chilled fresh fruit

soup

6	Serves
10 minutes, plus chilling	Preparation time
290	Kcal
1250	KJ
3 g	Protein
1 g	Fat
73 g	CHO

2 dessert apples, peeled, quartered
and cored

6 bananas, roughly chopped

500 g/1 lb fresh strawberries

375 g/12 oz pears, peeled,
quartered and cored

1 litre/1¾ pints fresh orange juice

2 tablespoons lemon juice

300 ml/½ pint fresh grapefruit juice

5–6 tablespoons clear honey

to garnish:

mint sprigs

6 strawberries

black pepper (optional)

1 Place all the fruit in a food processor or blender with 300 ml/½ pint of the orange juice and blend until very smooth. Add the lemon juice and grapefruit juice and the honey. Blend again until the mixture is smooth, in batches if necessary.

2 Pour the soup into a large bowl, stir in the remaining orange juice and cover the bowl loosely. Chill in the refrigerator for 3–4 hours.

3 Pour the chilled soup into 6 chilled bowls and garnish each portion with a sprig of fresh mint and a strawberry. Mill over some black pepper, if liked.

On a hot summer's day, this healthy concoction of fruit, juices and honey is an ideal replacement for breakfast, or even lunch.

vichyssoise

Serves	**8**
Preparation time	**15** minutes, plus chilling
Cooking time	about **35** minutes
Kcal	**180**
KJ	**758**
Protein	**8** g
Fat	**5** g
CHO	**27** g

25 g/1 oz butter or margarine

1 kg/2 lb leeks, white part only,
   thinly sliced

1 onion, chopped

1 litre/1¾ pints Vegetable Stock
   (see page 11)

pinch of grated nutmeg

750 g/1½ lb old potatoes, cubed

900 ml/1½ pints semi-skimmed
   milk

salt and white pepper

2 tablespoons snipped chives,
   to garnish

1 Melt the butter or margarine in a pan. Add the leeks and onion and cook over a moderate heat for 5 minutes, stirring constantly. Do not allow the vegetables to change colour.

2 Add the stock, nutmeg and potatoes with salt and pepper to taste. Bring the mixture to the boil, lower the heat and cook, partially covered, for 25 minutes. Pour in the milk and simmer for 5–8 minutes more. Cool slightly.

3 Purée the mixture in batches in a food processor or blender until smooth, then rub it through a sieve into a bowl. Stir well and cover the bowl closely. Chill in the refrigerator for at least 3 hours. Just before serving, adjust the seasoning, adding more salt and pepper if required. Serve in chilled bowls, garnishing each portion with a generous sprinkling of snipped chives.

This sophisticated iced soup is made from humble ingredients: leeks and potatoes. It was created in the 1920s by Louis Diat, a French chef working in the United States. Vichyssoise can be prepared 24 hours in advance and must always be velvety smooth and well chilled.

avgolemono

6	Serves
about **10** minutes	Preparation time
25 minutes	Cooking time
60	Kcal
255	KJ
4 g	Protein
2 g	Fat
7 g	CHO

1.5 litres/2½ pints Chicken Stock (see page 11)

50 g/2 oz long-grain rice

2 eggs

2–3 tablespoons lemon juice

1 tablespoon chopped parsley (optional)

salt and pepper

1 Combine the stock, ½ teaspoon of salt and the rice in a saucepan. Bring the mixture to the boil. Stir, lower the heat, cover the pan and simmer for 20 minutes. Stir once more.

2 Beat the eggs in a small bowl, then whisk in the lemon juice. Add a ladleful of stock, beat, and then add another ladleful of stock and beat once more.

3 Bring the remaining stock and rice mixture back to the boil. Briefly remove the saucepan from the heat and add the egg and lemon mixture. Stir well, lower the heat and simmer for a further 2 minutes, adding salt and pepper to taste. Sprinkle in the parsley, if using. Serve at once in warmed bowls.

This is a simple but effective way of preparing the delicious egg and lemon soup from Greece.

cream of celery
and prawn soup

Serves	**6**
Preparation time	**3–5** minutes
Cooking time	**5** minutes
Kcal	**100**
KJ	**425**
Protein	**2** g
Fat	**5** g
CHO	**11** g

1 Mix the celery soup and milk in a saucepan. Add the paprika a little at a time, to taste, and white pepper. Bring to simmering point, stirring constantly, for 5 minutes, then take the pan off the heat.

300 g/10 oz can condensed cream of celery soup

300 ml/½ pint semi-skimmed milk

½ teaspoon paprika

½ teaspoon white pepper

2 tablespoons very low-fat natural yogurt

50 g/2 oz cooked peeled prawns, defrosted if frozen

snipped chives, to garnish

2 If serving the soup hot, stir in the yogurt and prawns and reheat gently for about 2 minutes. Do not boil. Serve in warmed bowls, garnishing each portion with snipped chives.

3 If serving the soup chilled, pour the soup into a bowl and leave to cool. Stir in the yogurt and prawns, cover the bowl and chill for at least 3 hours. Serve the soup in chilled bowls, garnishing each portion with snipped chives.

This fragrant, smooth soup may be served hot or chilled and takes only a few minutes to prepare.

red lentil soup

4	Serves
10 minutes	Preparation time
25–30 minutes	Cooking time
140	Kcal
600	KJ
10 g	Protein
1 g	Fat
25 g	CHO

250 g/8 oz split red lentils

1 leek, sliced

2 large carrots, sliced

1 celery stick, sliced

1 garlic clove, crushed (optional)

1 bay leaf

1.2 litres/2 pints Vegetable Stock
   (see page 11)

½ teaspoon cayenne pepper

pepper

to garnish:

very low-fat natural yogurt

snipped chives or finely chopped
   parsley

1 Place all the ingredients except the garnish in a large saucepan, bring to the boil, cover and simmer for 20–25 minutes or until the lentils and all the vegetables are tender.

2 Allow the soup to cool slightly and remove the bay leaf. Purée the soup in batches in a food processor or blender until smooth.

3 Return the soup to a clean saucepan, season with pepper, and heat through. To serve, transfer to warmed soup plates or bowls, garnishing each portion with a swirl of yogurt and a sprinkling of chives or parsley.

For a lentil and tomato soup, reduce the amount of vegetable stock to 600 ml/1 pint and add a 400 g/13 oz can of chopped tomatoes. Continue as in the main recipe.

vegetable
and pasta soup

Serves	**4**
Preparation time	**15** minutes
Cooking time	about **25** minutes
Kcal	**150**
KJ	**630**
Protein	**6** g
Fat	**1** g
CHO	**30** g

250 g/8 oz carrots, diced

250 g/8 oz courgettes, sliced

2 large celery sticks, chopped

1 large onion, finely chopped

125 g/4 oz cabbage, shredded

600 ml/1 pint Chicken Stock (see
  page 11)

300 ml/½ pint tomato juice

1 garlic clove, crushed

125 g/4 oz small dried pasta
  shapes

salt and pepper

1 Place all the vegetables in a saucepan with the stock, tomato juice and garlic. Bring to the boil, then reduce the heat, and skim off any scum that rises to the surface.

2 Add the pasta and season with salt and pepper. Cover the pan and simmer for 15–20 minutes or until all the vegetables and the pasta are tender.

3 Serve the soup piping hot in warmed individual soup bowls.

The Italian for small pasta shapes is pastina; use any small pasta shapes such as anellini, farfallette or orecchiette in the soup.

green minestrone

6	Serves
2 hours, plus soaking	Preparation time
about **2½** hours	Cooking time
175	Kcal
738	KJ
8 g	Protein
5 g	Fat
27 g	CHO

125 g/4 oz dried haricot beans,
  soaked overnight and drained

2 tablespoons olive oil

2 leeks, sliced

1 garlic clove, crushed

2 tablespoons chopped parsley

2 tablespoons chopped mixed
  herbs

1.8 litres/3 pints water

2 celery sticks, chopped

4 tomatoes, skinned and chopped

2 potatoes, diced

50 g/2 oz dried ditali or other small
  pasta shapes

125 g/4 oz fresh or frozen peas

salt and pepper

1 Place the beans in a saucepan with enough water to cover. Bring to the boil, then cook for 1½ hours or until tender, adding salt towards the end of the cooking time.

2 Heat the oil in a saucepan, add the leeks, garlic and half of the parsley and mixed herbs and cook for 10 minutes. Add the water, celery, tomatoes, potatoes and season with salt and pepper. Simmer for 30 minutes. Add the pasta, peas and haricot beans and simmer for a further 15 minutes until the pasta is al dente and the vegetables tender. Stir in the remaining parsley and mixed herbs and serve at once.

To save time, you could use canned haricot beans in this well known Italian soup.

italian pasta
and bean soup

Serves	**6**
Preparation time	**30** minutes, plus soaking
Cooking time	**2½–3** hours
Kcal	**327**
KJ	**1390**
Protein	**23** g
Fat	**4** g
CHO	**53** g

175 g/6 oz smoked bacon, rinded
and chopped, or lean salt pork,
rinded and diced

1 onion, finely chopped

1 carrot, finely chopped

1 celery stick, finely chopped

125 g/4 oz dried pinto beans,
soaked overnight and drained

125 g/4 oz dried haricot beans,
soaked overnight and drained

2 garlic cloves, crushed

1.5 litres/2½ pints Vegetable Stock
(see page 11)

1 small ham bone (knuckle)

250 g/8 oz dried tagliatelle, broken
into 4–5 cm/1½–2 inch pieces

2 tablespoons finely chopped
parsley

salt and pepper

1 Put the bacon or pork into a heavy saucepan and place it over a moderate heat until the fat runs. Increase the heat and continue cooking, stirring occasionally, until the bacon or pork is crisp. Remove with a slotted spoon and set aside.

2 Add the onion, carrot and celery to the pan. Cook for 10–15 minutes, stirring, until soft. Drain the beans and add to the pan with the garlic, bacon or pork and three-quarters of the stock. Bring to the boil, then add the bone, cover and simmer for 1½–2 hours until the beans are soft.

3 Remove the bone and cut the meat from it into cubes, discarding the skin and fat. Put the meat back into the soup and add the remaining stock. Bring back to the boil. Add the pasta and half the parsley and season to taste with salt and pepper. Cook for 10–15 minutes, stirring occasionally, until the pasta is al dente. Serve sprinkled with the remaining parsley.

Serve this healthy, warming peasant dish with warm Italian bread; ciabatta or focaccia would be ideal.

bean and
mushroom soup

6	Serves
2 hours, plus soaking	Preparation time
about **30** minutes	Cooking time
227	Kcal
962	KJ
15 g	Protein
5 g	Fat
33 g	CHO

1 Place the haricot and red kidney beans in separate saucepans, cover with cold water and bring to the boil. Simmer the haricot beans for 1½ hours and the kidney beans for 1 hour or until tender, adding salt towards the end of cooking.

125 g/4 oz dried haricot beans, soaked overnight and drained

125 g/4 oz dried red kidney beans, soaked overnight and drained

2 tablespoons oil

1 onion, sliced

1 garlic clove, crushed

125 g/4 oz button mushrooms, sliced

1.2 litres/2 pints Vegetable Stock (see page 11)

175 g/6 oz broad beans, shelled

50 g/2 oz dried pasta, such as radiatori

salt and pepper

2 Heat the oil in a large saucepan, add the onion and cook for about 5 minutes until soft. Add the garlic, mushrooms, vegetable stock, broad beans and season to taste with salt and pepper and simmer for 10 minutes. Stir in the pasta and the drained haricot and kidney beans and simmer for a further 15 minutes or until the pasta is al dente.

Choose broad beans with soft, tender pale green pods with a satiny 'bloom'. The beans inside should be small and not fully mature.

pasta
and lentil soup

Serves	**4**
Preparation time	**20** minutes, plus soaking
Cooking time	about **1** hour
Kcal	**387**
KJ	**1646**
Protein	**23** g
Fat	**2** g
CHO	**74** g

250 g/8 oz small dried lentils, soaked overnight

175 g/6 oz canned tomatoes

2 garlic cloves, cut into 3–4 pieces

small bunch of parsley, roughly chopped

250 g/8 oz dried pasta, such as tubetti or pasta mista

salt

1 Drain the lentils and put them into a large saucepan, with enough water to come about 5 cm/2 inches over them. Add 1 teaspoon salt, bring to the boil and simmer until almost tender. The cooking time can vary, depending on the quality and type of lentils used.

2 Meanwhile, purée the tomatoes in a food processor. Heat a wok and dry fry the garlic for 3–6 minutes, stirring constantly. Transfer to a shallow baking dish and place in a preheated oven, 180°C (350°F), Gas Mark 4, for about 6 minutes until soft. Return to a saucepan and add the tomatoes, half of the parsley and salt to taste. Simmer gently for about 10 minutes.

3 When the lentils are ready, pour in the sauce, adding a little more water if necessary, enough to cover the pasta, then bring to the boil and add the pasta. Cook for 10–12 minutes until the pasta is al dente. Serve garnished with the remaining parsley.

To save time, the lentils can be cooked and the sauce can be made the previous day, just add the cooked pasta before serving.

consommé
with small pasta

6	Serves
30 minutes, plus cooling	Preparation time
3¼ hours	Cooking time
214	Kcal
910	KJ
8 g	Protein
1 g	Fat
46 g	CHO

1 Put all the ingredients, except for the pasta and a sprig of parsley, into a large saucepan and add enough water to come three-quarters of the way up the sides of the pan. Bring to the boil and simmer very slowly for about 3 hours, topping up with more boiling water if the level falls below that of the meat.

2 carrots, sliced

1 celery stick, halved

1 potato, halved

1 ripe tomato, halved

1 onion, halved

small bunch of parsley

500 g/1 lb chicken pieces, with
   skin removed

400 g/13 oz brisket of beef

1 teaspoon salt

375 g/12 oz dried anellini or
   capellini pasta

2 Remove the chicken and beef from the pan and strain the consommé through a fine sieve into a bowl. Leave the soup to stand overnight and when it is completely cold skim the fat off the surface.

3 Return the strained consommé to a saucepan, bring to the boil and add the pasta. Cook for 10–12 minutes until the pasta is al dente. Garnish with the reserved parsley and serve.

Make the consommé the day before, so that it can cool completely and all the fat can be removed.

pasta in broth

Serves	**4**
Preparation time	**15** minutes
Cooking time	**1½–2½** hours
Kcal	**170**
KJ	**728**
Protein	**6** g
Fat	**1** g
CHO	**37** g

250 g/8 oz chicken pieces,
chopped, with skin removed

250 g/8 oz stewing beef, cubed

1.2 litres/2 pints water

1 carrot, roughly chopped

1 celery stick, chopped

1 large onion, studded with
4–6 cloves

1 garlic clove, halved

4–6 black peppercorns

1 bouquet garni

200 g/7 oz dried tiny soup pasta

salt and pepper

to garnish:
celery leaves

marjoram leaves

1 Put the chicken and beef in a large saucepan. Pour in the water and bring to the boil, skimming off any scum that rises to the surface.

2 Add the carrot, celery, onion, garlic, peppercorns and bouquet garni to the saucepan and season to taste. Bring back to the boil, then reduce the heat, half cover the saucepan and simmer very gently for 1–2 hours (the longer the stock is left to cook the more flavoursome the broth will be). Top up with more cold water from time to time if necessary.

3 Strain the stock through a fine sieve into a clean saucepan. Skim off any fat. Bring the stock to the boil and add the pasta. Cover the pan and boil for 10 minutes, or until the pasta is al dente. Taste and adjust the seasoning, if necessary. Serve the soup hot, garnished with celery leaves and marjoram leaves.

This soup can be frozen for up to 3 months; freeze, before the pasta is added, in an airtight container. Defrost in a refrigerator then reheat until boiling. Add the pasta and then continue as in the recipe.

watercress
and vermicelli soup

6	Serves
10 minutes	Preparation time
30 minutes	Cooking time
104	Kcal
432	KJ
3 g	Protein
5 g	Fat
12 g	CHO

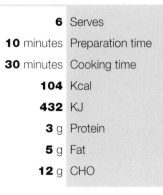

1 Heat the oil in a large saucepan, add the onion and watercress and cook gently for 5 minutes.

2 tablespoons vegetable oil

2 onions, sliced

2 bunches of watercress, roughly
   chopped

1.5 litres/2½ pints Chicken Stock
   (see page 11)

75 g/3 oz dried vermicelli, broken
   into short lengths

salt and pepper

1 egg, hard-boiled and finely
   chopped, to serve

2 Add the stock and season with salt and pepper, simmer for 20 minutes. Add the vermicelli and simmer for a further 5 minutes, or until the pasta is al dente. Serve sprinkled with chopped hard-boiled egg.

Watercress is rich in iron, calcium and vitamins A and C. It does not keep well so make this soup as soon as possible after buying the watercress.

chinese pork
and noodle soup

Serves	**4**
Preparation time	**15** minutes
Cooking time	**30** minutes
Kcal	**220**
KJ	**933**
Protein	**8** g
Fat	**5** g
CHO	**26** g

1.2 litres/2 pints Chicken Stock

(see page 11)

2 tablespoons light soy sauce

1 tablespoon vinegar

1 tablespoon medium dry sherry

250 g/8 oz lean pork fillet, cut

diagonally into 3.5 x 1 cm/1½ x

½ inch strips

3 spring onions, diagonally sliced

2.5 cm/1 inch piece of fresh root

ginger, peeled and cut into very

fine matchsticks

125 g/4 oz button mushrooms,

thinly sliced

200 g/7 oz Chinese leaves,

shredded

125 g/4 oz bean sprouts

125 g/4 oz medium egg noodles

salt and pepper

1 Place the stock in a large saucepan and bring it to the boil. Add the soy sauce, vinegar, sherry, pork strips, spring onions, ginger and mushrooms. Stir once, cover the pan and simmer for 10 minutes, stirring occasionally.

2 Add the Chinese leaves and cook for 5 minutes. Add the bean sprouts and noodles and season with salt and pepper to taste. Cook for 5 minutes more, or until the noodles are tender. Taste and adjust the seasoning, if necessary. Serve with some extra soy sauce, if liked.

The flavour of the chicken stock is important in this soup, so try to make your own if possible.

tomato, orange
and tarragon soup

8	Serves
15 minutes	Preparation time
30 minutes	Cooking time
65	Kcal
275	KJ
2 g	Protein
2 g	Fat
10 g	CHO

1 tablespoon vegetable oil

1 onion, sliced

175 g/6 oz potatoes, peeled and
   diced

1.75 kg/3½ lb tomatoes, chopped

2 tablespoons chopped fresh
   tarragon or 1 teaspoon dried
   tarragon

1 garlic clove, crushed

500 ml/17 fl oz Chicken Stock (see
   page 11)

250 ml/8 fl oz orange juice

1 teaspoon finely grated orange
   rind

salt and pepper

tarragon or parsley sprigs,
   to garnish

1 Heat the oil in a heavy saucepan over a medium-high heat. Sauté the onions and potatoes for 2–3 minutes, or until the onions are translucent.

2 Add the tomatoes, tarragon, garlic, stock and season with salt and pepper. Bring to the boil, then reduce the heat and simmer, covered, for 20–25 minutes, or until the vegetables are tender.

3 Purée the soup in a blender or food processor, then pass through a sieve and discard the pulp that remains in the sieve.

4 Mix the orange juice and rind into the soup. Reheat or serve chilled, garnished with fresh tarragon or parsley sprigs, if liked.

Establish your culinary reputation with this refreshing soup. It can be served hot or cold and is a sure winner.

spaghetti
with anchovies

Serves	**6**
Preparation time	**15** minutes
Cooking time	about **25** minutes
Kcal	**345**
KJ	**1463**
Protein	**15** g
Fat	**5** g
CHO	**64** g

500 g/1 lb dried spaghetti

2 x 50 g/2 oz cans anchovies in oil,
  drained

1 garlic clove, crushed

finely grated rind and juice of
  1 orange

pinch of sugar

½ tablespoon freshly grated
  Parmesan cheese

2 tablespoons chopped mint

salt and pepper

1 Bring a large saucepan of salted water to the boil. Add the spaghetti, stir and cook for 10–12 minutes until al dente.

2 Meanwhile, chop the anchovies and put them in a pan with the garlic over a moderate heat. Stir with a wooden spoon, pressing the anchovies so that they break up and become almost puréed. Add the orange rind and juice, the sugar and pepper to taste. Stir the sauce vigorously until heated through and combined with the anchovies.

3 Drain the spaghetti well and turn it into a warm serving bowl. Pour over the sauce, add the Parmesan and half the mint and toss together quickly. Serve at once, sprinkled with the remaining mint.

spaghetti
with clam sauce

4	Serves
15 minutes	Preparation time
about **30** minutes	Cooking time
370	Kcal
1566	KJ
22 g	Protein
2 g	Fat
66 g	CHO

3 Meanwhile, bring a large saucepan of salted water to the boil. Add the spaghetti, stir and cook for 10–12 minutes until al dente.

1 Place the canned tomatoes with their juice in a food processor or blender. Add the wine and herbs and work to a purée.

2 Heat a wok or heavy saucepan and dry fry the onion for 3–6 minutes, turning constantly. Add the garlic and puréed tomatoes. Season to taste. Cover and simmer gently for about 15 minutes, stirring occasionally.

4 Stir the clams into the tomato sauce and heat them through. Adjust the seasoning if necessary. Drain the spaghetti well and turn it into a warmed serving bowl. Pour over the sauce and garnish with chopped parsley. Serve at once.

400 g/13 oz can tomatoes

4 tablespoons dry red or white wine

2 tablespoons finely chopped parsley

2 teaspoons finely chopped basil

1 small onion, finely chopped

2 garlic cloves, crushed

250–300 g/8–10 oz dried spaghetti

300 g/10 oz can baby clams, well drained

salt and pepper

chopped parsley, to garnish

The Italian for this dish is *Spaghetti alle Vongole*. It is traditionally made with small fresh clams but using canned clams makes this a speedy dish.

tagliatelle romana

Serves	**4**
Preparation time	**30** minutes
Cooking time	**10–12** minutes
Kcal	**258**
KJ	**1096**
Protein	**16** g
Fat	**2** g
CHO	**48** g

1 Put the chicken stock into a large saucepan and bring to the boil. Add the tagliatelle, stir and cook for 10–12 minutes until just al dente, then drain and turn into a warmed serving dish.

1.5 litres/2½ pints Chicken Stock
   (see page 11)
250 g/8 oz dried tagliatelle
125 g/4 oz quark cheese
1 garlic clove, crushed
50 g/2 oz smoked prosciutto, fat
   removed, cut into strips
salt and pepper
finely chopped parsley, to garnish

2 Sieve the quark and mix in the garlic and seasoning. Stir the cheese mixture into the tagliatelle, toss in the strips of prosciutto, garnish with parsley and serve immediately.

Quark is a fresh curd cheese from Germany. The variety made with skimmed milk is lower in fat.

chilled stuffed
artichokes

4	Serves
20 minutes, plus cooling	Preparation time
about **35** minutes	Cooking time
133	Kcal
558	KJ
9 g	Protein
3 g	Fat
17 g	CHO

4 artichokes, stems **trimmed and
top third of leaves removed**

1 tablespoon lemon juice

**Steamed Vegetables with Ginger
(see right)**

sauce:

150 g/5 oz tofu, drained

4 tablespoons tomato purée

4 tablespoons horseradish sauce

2 teaspoons lemon juice

2 teaspoons white vinegar

½ teaspoon onion salt

½ teaspoon sugar

few drops Tabasco sauce

½ teaspoon grated lemon rind

**freshly ground white pepper, to
taste**

1 Place the artichokes and lemon juice in a deep saucepan and add boiling water to cover. Cover and cook for 30 minutes, or until one of the artichoke leaves pulls off easily. Remove from the pan, turn upside down to drain, then refrigerate to cool.

2 Remove the central choke of each artichoke and fill with chilled Steamed Vegetables with Ginger (see below).

3 To make the sauce, place all the ingredients in a blender or food processor and purée. Pour some sauce over each artichoke to serve.

steamed vegetables with ginger:

Place 3 carrots, cut into rounds, 4 tablespoons tomato purée, 75 g/ 3 oz each caluliflower and broccoli florets, 2 small courgettes, cut into rounds, and 3.5 cm/1½ inch piece root ginger, peeled and cut into thin strips, in a medium saucepan and steam for 7 minutes until tender.

meat and

Lean cuts of meat and poultry can be simply grilled for quick, low-fat meals. What makes these dishes special is an imaginative use of herbs, spices and flavourings.

chicken dishes

chicken and pasta

twist bake

Serves	**4**
Preparation time	about **10** minutes
Cooking time	about **30** minutes
Kcal	**380**
KJ	**1597**
Protein	**28** g
Fat	**3** g
CHO	**63** g

600 ml/1 pint skimmed milk

40 g/1½ oz plain flour, sieved

200 g/7 oz dried tri-colour pasta twists

250 g/8 oz boneless, skinless chicken breast, cooked and diced

50 g/2 oz fresh wholemeal breadcrumbs

salt and pepper

1 Place the milk and flour in a saucepan and bring to the boil over a gentle heat, stirring constantly until the sauce thickens. Simmer for 1 further minute, stirring frequently, then season generously with salt and pepper.

2 Meanwhile, cook the pasta twists in a large pan of boiling water for 10–12 minutes until al dente. Drain well.

3 Stir the chicken into the sauce and pour into a 2.5 litre/4 pint shallow ovenproof dish. Spoon the pasta twists over the sauce, pressing them in lightly, without submerging them completely. Sprinkle the breadcrumbs over the top of the pasta and bake in a preheated oven, 190°C (375° F), Gas Mark 5, for about 20 minutes until the breadcrumbs are golden and crisp. Serve hot.

Serve this pasta bake with a crisp green salad.

chicken olives
with orange and nut stuffing

6	Serves
about **20** minutes	Preparation time
30–35 minutes	Cooking time
140	Kcal
590	KJ
14 g	Protein
5 g	Fat
11 g	CHO

3 Roll up securely and tie with strong cotton or fine string. Put the chicken olives in a shallow pan and add the stock and orange juice. Cover, bring to the boil and simmer for 25–30 minutes until the chicken is just tender.

4 Remove the chicken olives with a slotted spoon and keep warm on a serving dish. Remove the string. Boil the cooking liquid until reduced by half. Spoon the cooking liquid over the chicken olives and garnish with rosemary sprigs and orange segments.

1 Lay the chicken breasts between dampened sheets of greaseproof paper and beat gently with a meat mallet or rolling pin.

2 Mix the orange rind with the breadcrumbs, onion, rosemary, walnuts and salt and pepper to taste and bind together with the egg white. Spread the mixture evenly over each chicken breast.

4 chicken breasts, about 75 g/3 oz
each, skinned, boned and halved
finely grated rind of 1 orange
4 tablespoons fresh wholemeal
breadcrumbs
1 small onion, finely chopped
2 tablespoons chopped rosemary
1 tablespoon chopped walnuts
1 egg white
150 ml/¼ pint Chicken Stock
(see page 11)
150 ml/¼ pint fresh orange juice
salt and pepper

to garnish:
rosemary sprigs
peeled orange segments

Make a lemon version of this recipe by replacing the orange rind with the finely grated rind of 2 lemons. Replace the fresh orange juice with the same quantity of fresh lemon juice. Garnish with lemon slices.

spinach
and chicken cannelloni

Serves	**6**
Preparation time	**20** minutes
Cooking time	**1¼** hours
Kcal	**440**
KJ	**1864**
Protein	**29** g
Fat	**5** g
CHO	**73** g

12 dried cannelloni tubes

25 g/1 oz half-fat Cheddar cheese, grated

filling:

250 g/8 oz fresh leaf spinach, washed

2 onions, finely chopped

150 g/5 oz cooked chicken breast, minced

125 g/4 oz low-fat cottage cheese

1 teaspoon ground cinnamon

salt and pepper

tomato sauce:

1 tablespoon chopped oregano

300 ml/½ pint passata (sieved tomatoes)

½ teaspoon caster sugar

cheese sauce:

15 g/½ oz cornflour

300 ml/½ pint skimmed milk

50 g/2 oz low-fat Cheddar cheese, grated

1 To prepare the filling, remove any tough stalks from the spinach and put it into a large saucepan with just the water that clings to the leaves. Cook over a low heat for 5 minutes or until the leaves have wilted. Strain the spinach and squeeze out all the excess liquid. Chop the spinach finely and transfer it to a bowl.

2 Heat a large frying pan or wok and dry fry the onion for 3–6 minutes, stirring constantly, until soft. Add half of the onion to the spinach with the chicken, cheese and cinnamon, and season to taste. Stir well and spoon into the cannelloni tubes, then arrange them in a single layer in a rectangular 1.2 litre/2 pint ovenproof dish.

3 To make the tomato sauce, transfer the remaining onion to a saucepan and stir in the oregano, passata and sugar and simmer for 15 minutes.

4 To make the cheese sauce, mix the cornflour with a little milk, heat the remaining milk in a saucepan and then mix in the cornflour mixture. Simmer until thickened. Add the cheese and stir until melted.

5 Pour the tomato sauce over the filled cannelloni, followed by the cheese sauce. Sprinkle the grated cheese over the top. Bake in a preheated oven, 190ºC (375ºF), Gas Mark 5, for 45 minutes. Serve at once.

lemon chicken

4	Serves
15 minutes	Preparation time
30–35 minutes	Cooking time
150	Kcal
630	KJ
17 g	Protein
5 g	Fat
9 g	CHO

1 tablespoon olive oil

1 small onion, thinly sliced

4 skinless, boneless chicken
   breasts, about 75 g/3 oz each

2 tablespoons chopped parsley

300 ml/½ pint Chicken Stock (see
   page 11)

1 tablespoon clear honey

4 tablespoons lemon juice

2 teaspoons cornflour

1 tablespoon water

rind of 1 lemon, cut into matchstick
   strips

salt and pepper

1 Heat the oil in a large frying pan. Add the onion and fry gently for 3–4 minutes. Add the chicken breasts and fry until lightly browned all over.

2 Add the parsley, stock, honey, salt and pepper to taste and lemon juice. Cover the pan and simmer gently for 20 minutes.

3 Using a slotted spoon remove the chicken breasts to a warmed serving dish, and keep warm.

4 Blend the cornflour and water to a smooth paste, stir in the hot cooking liquid, and then return to the pan. Stir over a gentle heat until thickened. Add the strips of rind to the sauce and spoon evenly over the chicken.

Serve this delicious citrus dish with a selection of steamed vegetables.

chicken fajitas

Serves **6**

Preparation time **15** minutes, plus marinating

Cooking time about **10** minutes

Kcal **300**

KJ **1270**

Protein **29** g

Fat **5** g

CHO **34** g

625 g/1¼ lb skinless, boneless
chicken breasts, cut into thin
strips

2 teaspoons vegetable oil

1 large onion, cut into thin strips

1 large green pepper, cored,
deseeded and cut into thin strips

8 flour tortillas

marinade:

1 garlic clove, finely chopped

1 tablespoon vegetable oil

1½ tablespoons lemon or lime juice

3 tablespoons Worcestershire
sauce

⅛ teaspoon pepper

1 To make the marinade, combine the garlic, oil, lemon or lime juice, Worcestershire sauce and pepper in a bowl. Add the chicken, toss to coat evenly and leave in the refrigerator for 10–20 minutes, turning at least once.

2 Heat the oil in a frying pan over a medium-high heat. Add the onion and green pepper and sauté, stirring constantly, for about 5 minutes, or until the onion is slightly brown. Remove from the heat and keep warm.

3 Wrap the tortillas in foil and place on the lower shelf of a preheated oven.

4 Line the grill pan with foil. Place the chicken strips on the foil and grill about 7 cm/3 inches from the heat for 4 minutes, turning once.

5 To serve, place 3 chicken strips on each tortilla and top with the onion, green peppers and assorted garnishes as desired (see below). Roll the tortilla around the chicken strips and eat it with your fingers.

This delicious dish is fun to make and good for you, too. Enjoy it with shredded lettuce, sliced tomatoes, salsa and guacamole, if you like.

green chilli
chicken with spinach taglioni

4	Serves
10 minutes	Preparation time
20 minutes	Cooking time
335	Kcal
1423	KJ
25 g	Protein
5 g	Fat
50 g	CHO

1 Cut each chicken breast into 4 pieces. Heat a wok or large frying pan and add the oil; when it is hot, add the chicken pieces, chillies and green pepper. Stir-fry for about 5 minutes or until the chicken has browned.

2 Stir in the lime juice, tomatoes and olives, with salt and pepper to taste. Reduce the heat and simmer the sauce for 15 minutes.

3 Meanwhile, bring a large saucepan of salted water to the boil. Add the pasta, stir and cook for about 10–12 minutes, until al dente.

4 Drain the pasta. Pile it on to a large warmed platter and spoon over the chicken mixture. Garnish with flat leaf parsley sprigs and serve at once.

4 boneless, skinless chicken
  breasts, each about 75 g/3 oz

1 teaspoon olive oil

2 green chillies, deseeded and
  sliced

1 green pepper, cored, deseeded
  and sliced

1 teaspoon lime juice

400 g/13 oz can chopped tomatoes

15 g/½ oz pitted black olives

15 g/½ oz pitted green olives

250 g/8 oz dried spinach taglioni

salt and pepper

flat leaf parsley sprigs, to garnish

To remove the seeds from the chillies; cut the chilli in half lengthways with a small, sharp knife and scrape out the seeds. For a hotter dish, leave the seeds in place.

chicken
and orange shells

Serves	**4**
Preparation time	**10** minutes
Cooking time	**15** minutes
Kcal	**434**
KJ	**1841**
Protein	**26** g
Fat	**5** g
CHO	**76** g

150 g/5 oz cooked chicken breast, roughly chopped

grated rind of 1 orange

2 tablespoons orange juice

1 egg, separated

3 tablespoons very low-fat natural yogurt

½ teaspoon cayenne pepper

16 large dried pasta shells, cooked

mixed salad leaves

salt and pepper

1 Combine the chicken, orange rind, juice, egg yolk, yogurt and cayenne in a food processor. Add salt and pepper to taste and process for 1 minute or until smooth. Whisk the egg white in a grease-free bowl until firm peaks form then fold into the chicken mixture.

2 Spoon a little of the filling into each pasta shell. Arrange the shells in a steamer and steam for 15 minutes or until the chicken filling has set.

3 Arrange the salad leaves on 4 serving plates and place the shells on top. Serve at once.

Serve the pasta shells with a fresh tomato sauce instead of the salad leaves, if you like.

turkey
and parma ham kebabs

4	Serves
20 minutes, plus marinating	Preparation time
about **10** minutes	Cooking time
187	Kcal
788	KJ
33 g	Protein
5 g	Fat
2 g	CHO

1 Put the turkey cubes into a shallow dish. Mix the lemon rind with the onion, garlic, pesto, basil and garlic oil, and salt and pepper to taste. Stir into the turkey, cover and chill for 3–4 hours.

2 Drain the turkey, reserving the marinade. Wrap each piece of turkey in a strip of Parma ham. Thread the turkey and ham rolls on kebab skewers, alternating with the mushrooms, bay leaves and wedges of lemon.

3 Brush the threaded skewers with the reserved marinade. Grill for 4–5 minutes. Turn the kebab skewers, brush once again with the marinade, and grill for a further 4–5 minutes.

4 Serve piping hot on a bed of shredded lettuce.

500 g/1 lb turkey fillet, cut into
   4 cm/1½ inch cubes

grated rind of 1 lemon

1 small onion, finely chopped

1 garlic clove, finely chopped

1 teaspoon pesto

1 tablespoon Basil and Garlic Oil
   (see right)

75 g/3 oz Parma ham, cut into long
   strips

8 small button mushrooms

8 small bay leaves

8 wedges of lemon

salt and pepper

shredded lettuce, to serve

basil and garlic oil:

1 Peel 4 large garlic cloves and bruise them with the back of a spoon. Put them into a bottle with 2 tablespoons chopped basil, 1 teaspoon black peppercorns and 600 ml/1 pint extra virgin olive oil. Firmly secure the bottle with a stopper and shake well. Store the oil in a cool place for 1 week before using.

For chicken kebabs, use boneless chicken breast instead of turkey fillet.

stir-fried beef
with peppers

Serves	**6**
Preparation time	**5** minutes
Cooking time	**10–12** minutes
Kcal	**130**
KJ	**550**
Protein	**16** g
Fat	**5** g
CHO	**3** g

1 tablespoon olive oil

1 onion, thinly sliced

1 large garlic clove, cut into thin
strips

500 g/1 lb fillet steak, cut into thin
strips

1 red pepper, cored, deseeded and
cut into matchstick strips

1 green pepper, cored, deseeded
and cut into matchstick strips

1 tablespoon soy sauce

2 tablespoons dry sherry

1 tablespoon chopped rosemary

salt and pepper

1 Heat the olive oil in a wok or deep frying pan and stir-fry the onion and garlic for 2 minutes.

2 Add the strips of beef and stir-fry briskly until evenly browned on all sides and almost tender.

3 Add the strips of red and green pepper and stir-fry for a further 2 minutes.

4 Add the soy sauce, sherry, salt and pepper to taste and the rosemary, and stir-fry for a further 1–2 minutes. Serve piping hot.

Serve with brown rice or egg noodles
for a satisfying meal.

sirloin steaks
with tomato-garlic sauce

4	Serves
10 minutes	Preparation time
about **20** minutes	Cooking time
140	Kcal
590	KJ
15 g	Protein
5 g	Fat
6 g	CHO

1 Heat the grill to high. Beat the steaks with a meat mallet or rolling pin until fairly thin, then spread with the low-fat spread. Place the steaks on the grill rack and grill for 8–10 minutes, or until cooked to your liking, turning them once.

2 Meanwhile, make the sauce. Place the tomatoes, garlic, basil and salt and pepper in a saucepan and simmer gently for about 10 minutes, until the tomatoes are soft.

3 Transfer the steaks to a heated serving dish and pour over the sauce. Serve immediately, garnished with the basil.

4 sirloin steaks, about 50 g/2 oz
  each, trimmed

2 teaspoons low-fat spread

basil sprigs, to garnish

tomato-garlic sauce:

750 g/1½ lb tomatoes, skinned and
  chopped

3 garlic cloves, crushed

1 tablespoon chopped basil

salt and pepper

Steamed French beans or mangetout are a good accompaniment to this tasty dish.

chinese pork
with bamboo shoots

Serves	**4**
Preparation time	**15** minutes
Cooking time	**20** minutes
Kcal	**219**
KJ	**913**
Protein	**19** g
Fat	**14** g
CHO	**6** g

2 tablespoons groundnut oil

300 g/10 oz lean pork, shredded

1 small Chinese cabbage, shredded

**1 tablespoon coarsely chopped
 hazelnuts**

**250 g/8 oz bamboo shoots, drained
 and sliced, with juices reserved**

2 tablespoons soy sauce

1 teaspoon curry powder

pinch of chilli powder

small pinch of sugar

salt and pepper

1 Heat the oil in a non-stick frying pan or wok, add the pork and stir-fry quickly until lightly browned. Season with salt and pepper to taste.

2 Add the cabbage, nuts and a few tablespoons of liquid from the can of bamboo shoots. Cook, stirring, for about 5 minutes.

3 Add the bamboo shoots, soy sauce, curry powder, chilli powder and sugar and mix well. Cook gently for a further 10 minutes. Serve immediately.

Bamboo shoots are a popular ingredient in Chinese dishes. In China, raw shoots are used, but the canned variety are a good substitute.

pork casserole

4	Serves
10 minutes	Preparation time
35–40 minutes	Cooking time
290	Kcal
1247	KJ
27 g	Protein
5 g	Fat
35 g	CHO

1 Trim away any visible fat from the pork. Place the meat in a saucepan with the onion, carrot, potatoes, stock and bay leaves. Bring to the boil, cover and simmer for about 30 minutes, or until the meat is tender.

2 Add the peas and beans. Blend the cornflour with the water and stir into the casserole. Bring back to the boil, then cover and simmer for a further 5 minutes, stirring occasionally.

3 To serve, remove the bay leaves and season the casserole with salt and pepper.

375 g/12 oz lean pork, diced

1 onion, sliced

150 g/5 oz carrots, sliced

500 g/1 lb baby new potatoes

400 ml/14 fl oz Vegetable Stock
  (see page 11)

2 bay leaves

125 g/4 oz frozen peas

75 g/3 oz green beans, trimmed

25 g/1 oz cornflour

50 ml/2 fl oz cold water

salt and pepper

Serve with plain boiled rice for a more substantial meal. This casserole could be made with any combination of vegetables; experiment with whatever you have to hand.

spaghetti
alla bolognese

Serves	**4**
Preparation time:	**15** minutes
Cooking time:	**35–40** minutes
Kcal	**558**
KJ	**2371**
Protein	**31** g
Fat	**5** g
CHO	**103** g

2 tablespoons Vegetable Stock (see page 11)

2 Spanish onions, chopped

1 tablespoon finely chopped rosemary

2 garlic cloves, crushed

2 x 400 g/13 oz cans chopped tomatoes

5 tablespoons tomato purée

½ teaspoon sugar

250 g/8 oz lean minced beef

500g/1 lb dried spaghetti

salt and pepper

1 Heat the stock in a saucepan, add the onions and cook until soft. Add the rosemary and garlic and cook gently for 1 minute. Stir in the tomatoes, tomato purée, sugar and salt and pepper to taste. Simmer for 10–15 minutes. Mix in the beef and stir until browned. Gently bring back to the boil and simmer for 20 minutes

2 Meanwhile, bring a large saucepan of salted water to the boil. Add the spaghetti, stir and cook for 10–12 minutes until al dente. Drain and season with pepper.

3 Divide the spaghetti among warmed plates. Ladle over the sauce and serve immediately.

Make sure that the mince is really lean; to be certain, ask your butcher to mince some steak for you.

stir-fried steak

and tagliatelle

4	Serves
15–20 minutes	Preparation time
15 minutes	Cooking time
518	Kcal
2202	KJ
28 g	Protein
5 g	Fat
96 g	CHO

1 Heat a large frying pan or wok over a moderate heat, add the garlic, ginger, onion and a pinch of salt and dry-fry for 2–3 minutes, turning constantly.

2 Add the steak and stir-fry for 2–3 minutes, until brown on all sides.

3 Add the broccoli and continue to stir-fry for 2 minutes. Add the mushrooms, soy sauce, stock and sugar and stir-fry for a further 3–4 minutes.

4 Meanwhile, bring a large saucepan of salted water to the boil. Add the pasta, stir and cook for 10–12 minutes until al dente. Drain the pasta, add to the wok and toss for a few more minutes to allow the pasta to absorb some of the juices. Add pepper to taste. Serve immediately.

1 garlic clove, crushed

1 teaspoon finely chopped fresh
   root ginger

25 g/1 oz onion, finely chopped

200 g/7 oz steak, cut into thin
   strips

175 g/6 oz broccoli florets, finely
   sliced

125 g/4 oz mushrooms, finely
   sliced

2 tablespoons light soy sauce

4 tablespoons Vegetable Stock (see
   page 11)

1 teaspoon caster sugar

500 g/1 lb dried tagliatelle

salt and pepper

The vegetables and meat are dry-fried to avoid adding extra fat to this healthy dish.

coriander and chive
meatballs

Serves	**6**
Preparation time	**20** minutes
Cooking time	about **30** minutes
Kcal	**283**
KJ	**1197**
Protein	**14** g
Fat	**5** g
CHO	**48** g

1 onion, grated

50 g/2 oz grated Parmesan cheese

150 g/5 oz lean minced beef

1 tablespoon tomato purée

1 teaspoon chilli sauce

1 bunch coriander, finely chopped

1 bunch chives, chopped

125 g/4 oz very finely chopped
mushrooms

2 teaspoons sunflower oil

375 g/12 oz dried spaghetti

salt and pepper

basil sprigs, to garnish

sauce:

1 onion, finely chopped

2 garlic cloves, crushed

400 g/13 oz can chopped tomatoes
with herbs

2 tablespoons tomato purée

2 tablespoons chopped oregano

1 To make the meatballs, combine the onion, Parmesan, minced beef, tomato purée, chilli sauce, herbs and mushrooms in a bowl. Add salt and pepper and mix thoroughly.

2 Using dampened hands, shape the mixture into small balls. Heat the oil in a frying pan and fry the meatballs, in batches, for about 10 minutes until browned. Using a slotted spoon, transfer the meatballs to a baking dish. Keep hot.

3 Bring a large pan of salted water to the boil. Add the pasta, stir and cook for 10–12 minutes, until al dente.

4 Meanwhile, make the sauce. Heat a wok or frying pan, add the onion and garlic and dry-fry for 3–6 minutes, stirring constantly, until soft and lightly browned. Stir in the tomatoes, tomato purée and oregano. Simmer for about 8 minutes.

5 Drain the pasta and pile it into a warmed bowl. Pour over the tomato sauce and toss lightly. Serve with the meatballs, garnished with basil sprigs.

Chestnut mushrooms can be used for this dish. They have a slightly stronger flavour than other cultivated mushrooms and are light brown in colour.

beef
and mangetout stir-fry

4	Serves
10 minutes, plus marinating	Preparation time
8 mins	Cooking time
348	Kcal
1475	KJ
27 g	Protein
5 g	Fat
50 g	CHO

25 g/1 oz fresh root ginger, peeled

  and shredded

1 garlic clove, crushed

4 tablespoons light soy sauce

2 tablespoons dry sherry

1 teaspoon chilli sauce

1 teaspoon clear honey

½ teaspoon Chinese five-spice

  powder

375 g/12 oz fillet steak, finely

  sliced

250 g/8 oz dried low-fat egg

  noodles

250 g/8 oz mangetout, trimmed

salt and pepper

shredded spring onions, to garnish

1 Combine the ginger, garlic, soy sauce, sherry, chilli sauce, honey and five-spice powder in a non-metallic bowl. Stir well. Add the steak, stir to coat thoroughly, then cover and marinate for at least 30 minutes.

2 Bring a large saucepan of lightly salted water to the boil. Add the noodles, remove the pan from the heat, cover and leave to stand for 5 minutes.

3 Meanwhile, heat a wok or frying pan. Add 2 tablespoons of the marinade and the beef and stir-fry for about 3–6 minutes.

4 Add the mangetout and the remaining marinade to the wok, with salt and pepper if required. Stir-fry for a further 2 minutes.

5 Drain the noodles and arrange them in warmed serving bowls. Spoon the stir-fry over the top, garnish with shredded spring onions and serve.

Sugar snap peas can be used instead of the mangetout; they have a more rounded pod and sweeter flavour.

pork fillet
with grapefruit sauce

Serves	**6**
Preparation time	**15** minutes, plus marinating
Cooking time	about **10** minutes
Kcal	**100**
KJ	**430**
Protein	**8** g
Fat	**4** g
CHO	**9** g

250 g/8 oz pork fillet, cut into
    5 mm/¼ inch thick medallions

3 spring onions, finely chopped

finely grated rind and juice of
    ½ grapefruit

1 teaspoon soft light brown sugar

2 tablespoons chopped parsley

1 tablespoon olive oil

150 ml/¼ pint unsweetened apple
    purée (see below)

150 ml/¼ pint Chicken Stock (see
    page 11)

2 grapefruit, peeled and divided
    into segments, pith and
    membrane removed

salt and pepper

1 Place the pork medallions in a shallow dish with the spring onions, grapefruit rind and juice, brown sugar, salt and pepper to taste, and the parsley. Turn to coat well. Cover and chill for 3–4 hours.

2 Drain the pork medallions, reserving the marinade. Heat the oil in a frying pan and fry the medallions briskly until sealed on all sides.

3 Mix the apple purée with the stock and reserved marinade and pour over the pork. Cover and simmer for about 7 minutes until the pork is tender. Stir in the grapefruit segments and heat through.

To make the apple purée, put 500 g/1lb peeled, cored and sliced cooking apples into a saucepan with 2 tablespoons of water. Cover and cook until they form a purée. Beat or liquidize until smooth.

tagliatelle riviera

4	Serves
10 minutes	Preparation time
about **20** minutes	Cooking time
478	Kcal
2030	KJ
18 g	Protein
5 g	Fat
95 g	CHO

2 teaspoons olive oil

2 onions, sliced

2 garlic cloves, crushed

2 slices lean bacon, rinded and

   chopped

250 g/8 oz mushrooms, sliced

2 anchovy fillets, chopped

6 pitted black olives, halved

500 g/1 lb dried tagliatelle

salt and pepper

basil leaves, to garnish

1 Heat the oil in a frying pan. Add the onions, garlic and bacon and fry until the onions are soft but not brown. Stir in the mushrooms, anchovy fillets, olives and salt and pepper to taste. Cook for a further 4–5 minutes or until very hot.

2 Meanwhile, bring a large saucepan of salted water to the boil. Add the pasta, stir and cook for 10–12 minutes until al dente. Drain the tagliatelle and arrange in a warmed bowl. To serve, spoon over the sauce and garnish with the basil leaves.

A delicious accompaniment to this dish is a fresh rocket and basil salad, lightly tossed with balsamic vinegar.

fish

Fish needs only simple preparation and a few extra ingredients to make a really exciting meal. It cooks quickly and is naturally low in fat and high in flavour.

dishes

poached salmon
with hot basil sauce

Serves	**4**
Preparation time	**20** minutes
Cooking time	**40–50** minutes
Kcal	**170**
KJ	**710**
Protein	**12** g
Fat	**11** g
CHO	**4** g

1 large bunch of fresh basil

2 celery sticks, chopped

1 carrot, chopped

1 small courgette, chopped

1 small onion, chopped

4 salmon steaks, about
**   50 g/2 oz each**

75 ml/3 fl oz white wine

125 ml/4 fl oz water

1 teaspoon lemon juice

15 g/½ oz unsalted butter

salt and pepper

basil sprigs, to garnish

1 Strip the leaves off half the basil and set aside.

2 Spread the chopped celery, carrot, courgette and onion evenly over the bottom of a large flameproof dish or pan with a lid, place the salmon steaks on top and cover them with the remaining basil.

3 Pour over the wine and water and add salt and pepper to taste. Bring to the boil, cover and simmer for about 10 minutes. Transfer the salmon to a warmed serving dish.

4 Bring the poaching liquid and vegetables back to the boil and simmer for 5 minutes. Strain into a blender or food processor and add the cooked and uncooked basil. Blend to a purée and transfer to a saucepan.

5 Bring the purée to the boil and reduce by half to thicken.

6 Remove the pan from the heat, add the lemon juice and stir in the butter. Pour the sauce over the salmon steaks and serve, garnished with basil sprigs.

Serve this delicious dish with steamed new potatoes and mangetout or sugar snap peas.

piquant plaice
paupiettes

4	Serves
20 minutes	Preparation time
13 minutes	Cooking time
185	Kcal
784	KJ
23 g	Protein
3 g	Fat
11 g	CHO

1 Lay out the plaice fillets skinned sides uppermost and sprinkle with salt, pepper and ground ginger. Roll up and secure with wooden cocktail sticks.

8 skinned plaice fillets, about 50 g/2 oz each

¼ teaspoon ground ginger

1 small onion, finely chopped

150 ml/¼ pint white wine

150 ml/¼ pint Fish or Chicken Stock (see page 11)

2 leeks, cut into matchstick strips

4 tablespoons very low-fat natural yogurt

1 thin slice fresh root ginger, peeled

½ teaspoon mild curry powder

salt and pepper

small croûtons, to garnish

2 Scatter the onion in a large frying pan, lay the plaice on top and add the white wine and stock. Cover the pan and simmer gently for about 10 minutes. Remove the plaice paupiettes with a slotted spoon and keep warm.

3 Meanwhile, simmer the strips of leek in boiling water for 3 minutes, then drain.

4 Put the yogurt into a bowl. Squeeze the fresh ginger in a garlic press to extract the juice and add to the yogurt with the curry powder and seasoning.

5 Arrange 2 paupiettes on each plate and garnish with the strips of leek and croûtons. Serve the sauce separately.

Make sure that you toast the croûtons rather than fry them. Use small shaped cutters to make decorative croûtons.

trout in a paper bag

Serves **4**

Preparation time: **30** minutes

Cooking time: **20** minutes

Kcal **160**

KJ **680**

Protein **23** g

Fat **5** g

CHO **1** g

4 trout, about 125 g/4 oz each

2 garlic cloves, finely chopped

1 tablespoon chopped thyme

1 tablespoon chopped rosemary

150 ml/¼ pint rosé wine

salt and pepper

1 Cut 8 rectangles of greaseproof paper or kitchen foil, double the width of each trout, and half as long again as the fish.

2 Place 4 of the rectangles on a baking sheet. Lay a trout along the centre of each one, pull up the edges of the paper or foil and fold at each corner so that the paper forms a container for each fish.

3 Sprinkle a little salt and pepper, garlic and herbs over each trout, then spoon 2 tablespoons of the rosé wine over each one. Cover loosely with the remaining paper or foil and fold at the corners as before to form a lid over each fish. Fold the top and bottom layers of paper or foil together in several places. Bake the trout in a preheated oven, 190°C (375°F), Gas Mark 5, for 20 minutes, until the fish is cooked.

4 Take the fish to the table in the parcels to serve.

Thinly sliced courgettes, flavoured with crushed garlic and chopped fennel, can be wrapped in individual foil parcels and cooked with the fish. They make a delicious accompaniment.

fillets of sole
with melon and mint sauce

4	Serves
20 minutes	Preparation time
10–12 minutes	Cooking time
230	Kcal
985	KJ
29 g	Protein
3 g	Fat
12 g	CHO

4 sole fillets, halved

2 tablespoons chopped mint

300 ml/½ pint dry white wine

1 Charentais melon, halved and
   seeded

150 ml/¼ pint natural yogurt

salt and pepper

mint sprigs, to garnish

1 Season the sole fillets with salt and pepper and sprinkle with half of the mint. Roll up each fish fillet and secure with wooden cocktail sticks. Place the fish rolls in a deep frying pan and sprinkle over the remaining mint. Add the white wine. Cover the pan and poach gently for about 8 minutes, until the fish is tender.

2 Meanwhile, using a Parisian cutter or melon ball cutter, scoop the melon flesh into small balls. Cut out any remaining melon flesh attached to the skin.

3 Carefully drain the rolled fillets, place on a warm serving dish and keep warm. Remove the cocktail sticks.

4 Boil the poaching liquid with the remnants of melon flesh until well reduced and whisk until smooth. If necessary, purée in a food processor or blender.

5 Stir in the yogurt and heat the sauce through gently. Season with salt and pepper and spoon over the cooked fish. Garnish with the melon balls and sprigs of mint.

Charentais melon is a type of cantaloupe with a roughish, pale green skin. It has a fragrant orange flesh when ripe. Mint complements melon very well.

pasta twists
with mussels

Serves	**4**
Preparation time	**1** hour
Cooking time	**30** minutes
Kcal	**428**
KJ	**1820**
Protein	**28** g
Fat	**4** g
CHO	**75** g

1 kg/2 lb live mussels

300 ml/½ pint water

150 ml/¼ pint dry white wine

1 bouquet garni

375 g/12 oz dried wholewheat
pasta twists, or other pasta
shapes

300 ml/½ pint very low-fat natural
yogurt

2 tablespoons chopped parsley

salt and pepper

lemon balm, to garnish

1 Prepare the mussels (see below). Put the mussels into a large saucepan with the water and wine, bring to the boil, cover the pan and steam for 5–6 minutes, or until the shells have opened. Drain the mussels and reserve the cooking liquid. Discard any unopened mussels.

2 Pour the mussel liquid into a saucepan, add the bouquet garni, bring to the boil and fast-boil for 10 minutes, or until reduced by two-thirds. Discard the bouquet garni.

3 Remove the mussels from their shells, leaving about 8 in the shell to use as a garnish.

4 Bring a large saucepan of salted water to the boil. Add the pasta, stir and cook for 12–14 minutes until al dente. Drain, refresh in hot water, then drain again.

5 Put the pasta and mussels into a saucepan and season with pepper. Toss well. Beat the reserved mussel liquid with the yogurt, stir in the parsley and pour over the pasta. Toss well. Turn the pasta into a warmed serving dish and garnish with lemon balm and the reserved mussels.

Use live mussels as soon as possible after purchase. To prepare, put the mussels in a large bowl and scrub off any sand or mud. Knock off any barnacles with a knife and pull off the 'beard'. Discard any mussels that remain open when tapped.

hoki
with light lemon sauce

4	Serves
20 minutes	Preparation time
15 minutes	Cooking time
190	Kcal
798	KJ
34 g	Protein
2 g	Fat
42 g	CHO

1 Place the hoki fillets in a large frying pan with the cold water and bring to the boil over gentle heat. Simmer for 5–10 minutes, depending on the thickness of the fish. The fish will be fully cooked when the flesh turns white and flakes when gently pressed. Using a fish slice, transfer the cooked fish to a warm serving dish, cover and keep warm.

4 hoki fillets, about 175 g/6 oz each

150 ml/¼ pint cold water

2 teaspoons cornflour

150 ml/¼ pint skimmed milk

125 g/4 oz very low-fat natural yogurt

2 teaspoons lemon juice

grated rind of 1 lemon

½ teaspoon granular low-calorie sweetener

parsley sprigs, to garnish

2 While the fish is cooking, blend the cornflour with the milk and place in a small saucepan. Bring to the boil, stirring constantly, to make a smooth, thick sauce. Reduce the heat and simmer gently for 3–4 minutes to cook the cornflour thoroughly, stirring from time to time.

3 Remove the sauce from the heat and carefully stir in the yogurt, lemon juice, half of the lemon rind and the low-calorie sweetener. Return to the heat to warm through, but do not allow the sauce to boil.

4 To serve, pour the warm sauce over the hoki fillets. Garnish with the remaining lemon rind and the sprigs of parsley.

Hoki is available at good fishmongers and larger supermarkets, although other white fish such as cod or haddock could be used instead.

fettucine
with prawn sauce

Serves	**4**
Preparation time	**15** minutes
Cooking time	about **20** minutes
Kcal	**579**
KJ	**2460**
Protein	**37** g
Fat	**4** g
CHO	**98** g

1 onion, chopped

2 garlic cloves, crushed

500 g/1 lb tomatoes, skinned and
   chopped (see below)

½ teaspoon dried basil

375 g/12 oz peeled raw prawns

150 ml/¼ pint white wine

2 tablespoons chopped parsley

500 g/1 lb dried fettucine

salt and pepper

1 Put the onion and garlic into a saucepan with a little water and simmer until soft.

2 Add the tomatoes and basil, season with salt and pepper and simmer gently for 5 minutes. Stir in the prawns, wine and parsley and simmer for a further 10 minutes.

3 Bring a large saucepan of salted water to the boil. Add the pasta, stir and cook for 10–12 minutes until al dente.

4 Drain the pasta and place on a warm serving dish. Pour over the prawn sauce and serve at once.

To skin tomatoes, place them in a heatproof bowl and pour over boiling water to cover. Leave for 1–2 minutes, then drain and cut a cross at the stem end of each tomato with a sharp knife. Carefully peel off the skins.

pasta with tuna
and tomato sauce

4	Serves
10 minutes	Preparation time
20–25 minutes	Cooking time
482	Kcal
1369	KJ
27 g	Protein
3 g	Fat
94 g	CHO

1 garlic clove, chopped

**200 g/7 oz can tuna in brine,
drained and coarsely flaked**

3 tablespoons chopped parsley

2 tablespoons tomato purée

**250 ml/8 fl oz Fish Stock (see
page 11)**

**500g/1 lb dried macaroni, rigatoni,
or penne**

salt and pepper

1 Heat a large frying pan or wok and dry fry the garlic for 3–6 minutes, turning constantly, until soft and just beginning to colour. Add the flaked tuna, 2 tablespoons of the parsley, the tomato purée and fish stock. Season to taste with salt and pepper. Simmer gently for 15 minutes.

2 Meanwhile, bring a large saucepan of salted water to the boil. Add the pasta, stir and cook for 10–12 minutes until al dente. Drain, mix with the tuna sauce and transfer to a serving dish.

3 Sprinkle with the remaining chopped parsley and serve at once.

This is a really quick supper dish which can be made from storecupboard ingredients.

baked trout parcels

Serves **2**
Preparation time **10–15** minutes
Cooking time **20** minutes
Kcal **150**
KJ **624**
Protein **22** g
Fat **4** g
CHO **4** g

2 garlic cloves, crushed

1 onion, chopped

1 celery stick, chopped

4 rosemary sprigs

2 tablespoons dry white wine

2 x 200 g/7 oz trout, cleaned

salt and pepper

rosemary sprigs, to garnish

1 Put the garlic, onion and celery in the top part of a steamer. Steam gently for about 5 minutes until soft and tender. Season with salt and pepper, add 2 of the rosemary sprigs and the dry white wine and cook gently for 5 minutes.

2 Cut out 2 double sheets of kitchen foil or greaseproof paper large enough to enclose the trout. Divide the onion mixture equally between the 2 pieces of paper.

3 Wash the trout and dry well with kitchen paper. Sprinkle inside and out with salt and pepper. Place one trout on top of the onion mixture on each piece of foil or paper and top with a sprig of rosemary.

4 Fold the foil or paper over the fish and wrap loosely, securing the sides with a double fold and double folding the ends. Place the parcels on a baking sheet and cook in a preheated oven, 180°C (350°F), Gas Mark 4, for 20 minutes or until the fish is cooked and tender. Remove the fish from the foil or paper and serve garnished with sprigs of rosemary.

For a variation, replace the celery with 50 g/2 oz chopped watercress and substitute dill for the rosemary. Follow the main recipe and serve garnished with dill.

noodles
with fish sauce

6	Serves
15 minutes, plus soaking	Preparation time
20–25 minutes	Cooking time
370	Kcal
1572	KJ
19 g	Protein
5 g	Fat
64 g	CHO

1 Wash the anchovies in water and dry with kitchen paper. Put them into a bowl with the milk and leave to soak for 30 minutes. Drain the anchovies, chop and set aside.

10 canned anchovy fillets

2–3 tablespoons skimmed milk

25 g/1 oz low-fat spread

1 large onion, chopped

2 garlic cloves, thinly sliced

150 ml/¼ pint dry white wine

250 ml/8 fl oz Fish Stock (see page 11)

175 g/6 oz cooked peeled prawns

2–3 tablespoons chopped parsley

500 g/1 lb fresh low-fat noodles

salt and pepper

to garnish:

anchovy fillets

whole prawns

2 Melt half of the low-fat spread in a saucepan, add the onion and cook for about 10 minutes, stirring, until golden brown. Add the garlic and cook for 1 minute. Add the wine, bring to the boil and cook rapidly until reduced by half. Add the fish stock, anchovies, prawns, and salt and pepper to taste and cook, uncovered, for 2 minutes. Remove the pan from the heat and stir in the parsley.

3 Bring a large saucepan of salted water to the boil. Add the noodles, stir and cook for 4–5 minutes until al dente. Drain thoroughly and turn into a warm serving dish. Add the remaining low-fat spread and toss well.

4 Reheat the sauce for 1 minute, then pour over the noodles and toss well. Garnish with anchovy fillets and whole prawns.

Try to use noodles made without eggs as these will be lower in fat. Wheat noodles are available without the addition of egg.

sole
and smoked salmon paupiettes

Serves **6**
Preparation time **15** minutes
Cooking time about **15** minutes
Kcal **114**
KJ **480**
Protein **23** g
Fat **2** g
CHO **0** g

6 skinned sole fillets, about
    50 g/2 oz each
3 slices smoked salmon, about
    25 g/1 oz each
1 tablespoon chopped dill
300 ml/½ pint Fish Stock (see
    page 11)
300 ml/½ pint Herb and Lemon
    Sauce (see right) (optional)
50 g/2 oz cooked peeled prawns
salt and pepper

to garnish:
dill sprigs
twists of lemon

1 Lay the sole fillets out flat and season with salt and pepper. Cut the slices of smoked salmon in half lengthways and lay a strip down the length of each sole fillet. Sprinkle with chopped dill and roll up loosely. Secure with wooden cocktail sticks.

2 Place the fish rolls in a shallow pan and add the fish stock. It should cover the fish. Cover and simmer for about 8 minutes until just tender. Drain the fish and keep warm on a serving dish.

3 Spoon 4 tablespoons of the fish cooking liquid into a small pan and boil quickly over a high heat until reduced to about 1 tablespoon.

4 Stir the herb and lemon sauce, if using, and the prawns into the reduced cooking liquid and heat through gently. Spoon the sauce evenly over the fish paupiettes and garnish with sprigs of fresh dill and twists of lemon.

These light paupiettes are delicious served with the herb and lemon sauce (right), but the fat content is then increased.

herb
and lemon sauce

300 ml/½ pint	Makes
10 minutes	Preparation time
185	Kcal
777	KJ
26 g	Protein
8 g	Fat
3 g	CHO

2 hard-boiled egg yolks

grated rind and juice of 1 lemon

1 teaspoon French mustard

1 teaspoon soft dark brown sugar

4 tablespoons Fish or Vegetable
   Stock (see page 11)

2 tablespoons olive oil

4 tablespoons low-fat natural
   yogurt

1 tablespoon each finely chopped
   tarragon, basil and parsley

salt and pepper

1 Mix the egg yolks to a paste with the lemon rind and juice, mustard and sugar.

2 Gradually beat in the stock, olive oil and yogurt.

3 Add the herbs, and salt and pepper to taste.

spaghetti
with sardines

Serves	**6**
Preparation time	**20** minutes
Cooking time	about **25–30** minutes
Kcal	**346**
KJ	**1469**
Protein	**16** g
Fat	**4** g
CHO	**69** g

1 onion, chopped

500 g/1 lb tomatoes, skinned and
  chopped

1 garlic clove, crushed

½ teaspoon saffron, soaked in
  4 tablespoons boiling water

150 g/5 oz can sardines in brine

500 g/1 lb dried spaghetti

salt and pepper

1 Heat a griddle pan or wok and dry-fry the onion, turning constantly for 3–6 minutes, until soft. Add the tomatoes, garlic, the saffron with its soaking water, sardines and salt and pepper to taste and simmer gently for 20 minutes.

2 Meanwhile, bring a large saucepan of salted water to the boil. Add the pasta, stir and cook for 10–12 minutes until al dente. Drain and mix with the sardine sauce. Serve immediately.

Tagliatelle can be used instead of the spaghetti. Serve this dish with Italian bread sticks and an Italian red wine.

pasta
with sea bass

4	Serves
30 minutes	Preparation time
30 minutes	Cooking time
406	Kcal
1720	KJ
34 g	Protein
5 g	Fat
59 g	CHO

1 Heat the oil in a frying pan and add the garlic, green pepper and onion. Stir constantly for about 5 minutes until softened. Add the tomatoes and their juice, lemon juice and basil and cook for a further 5 minutes, breaking up the tomatoes with a wooden spoon.

1 teaspoon olive oil

1 garlic clove, finely chopped

60 g/2½ oz green pepper, cored, deseeded and chopped

60 g/2½ oz onion, finely chopped

250 g/8 oz canned tomatoes

1 tablespoon lemon juice

1 tablespoon chopped basil

4 sea bass fillets, weighing 125 g/ 4 oz each

300 g/10 oz dried casareccie pasta

salt and pepper

2 Arrange the fillets in a single layer in a shallow baking dish and pour over the sauce. Cover the dish with foil and place in a preheated oven, 180°C (350°F), Gas Mark 4, and bake for about 15–20 minutes, or until the fish flakes easily.

3 Meanwhile, bring a large saucepan of lightly salted water to the boil. Add the pasta, stir and cook for 10–12 minutes until al dente.

4 Drain the pasta and turn into a warm serving dish. Add the flaked fish and its sauce, toss gently and serve at once.

Sea bass is a large round fish which grows up to 100 cm/40 inches long. It is easy to cook and has soft delicate flesh.

vegetable

The huge variety of fresh vegetables available nowadays provides an opportunity for delicious and unusual recipes. Many of the recipes here are suitable for vegetarians.

dishes

stir-fried vegetables

Serves **4**

Preparation time **15–20** minutes

Cooking time **3–5** minutes

Kcal **68**

KJ **280**

Protein **3** g

Fat **3** g

CHO **7** g

1 tablespoon vegetable oil

125 g/4 oz bamboo shoots, thinly
    sliced

125 g/4 oz mangetout

125 g/4 oz carrots, thinly sliced

50 g/2 oz broccoli florets

125 g/4 oz fresh bean sprouts,
    rinsed

1 teaspoon salt

1 teaspoon sugar

1 tablespoon Vegetable Stock (see
    page 11) or water

1 Heat the oil in a preheated wok
or frying pan. Add the bamboo
shoots, mangetout, carrots and
broccoli florets and stir-fry for
about 1 minute.

2 Add the bean sprouts with the
salt and sugar. Stir-fry for another
minute or so, then add some
stock or water if necessary. Do
not overcook or the vegetables
will lose their crunchiness. Serve
immediately.

Serve this colourful stir-fry with plain boiled rice or
low-fat noodles for a healthy accompaniment.

paglia e fieno
with tomato and rosemary

4	Serves
15 minutes	Preparation time
about **50** minutes	Cooking time
277	Kcal
1178	KJ
9 g	Protein
4 g	Fat
53 g	CHO

625 g/1¼ lb can tomatoes

1 tablespoon olive oil

1 small carrot, finely chopped

1 small onion, finely chopped

1 celery stick, finely chopped

about 4 tablespoons red wine

2 whole dried red chillies

250–300 g/8–10 oz fresh paglia
  e fieno pasta

2 teaspoons chopped rosemary

salt and pepper

rosemary sprigs, to garnish

1 Purée the tomatoes and their juice in a food processor or blender.

2 Heat the oil in a heavy saucepan. Add the carrot, onion and celery and cook gently, stirring frequently, for 15 minutes or until soft. Add the red wine, increase the heat and stir until the wine has been absorbed by the vegetables. Add the puréed tomatoes and the whole chillies, then season to taste and bring to the boil. Reduce the heat, cover, and simmer for 15–20 minutes until the sauce is quite thick.

3 Meanwhile, bring a large saucepan of salted water to the boil. Add the pasta, stir and cook for 3–4 minutes until al dente. Drain the pasta and turn it into a warmed bowl. Remove the sauce from the heat and stir in the chopped rosemary. Adjust the seasoning. Pour the sauce over the pasta and serve garnished with rosemary sprigs.

Dried chillies taste very hot, so it is best to remove them before serving.

penne
with spring vegetables

Serves	**4**
Preparation time	**10** minutes
Cooking time	about **25** minutes
Kcal	**457**
KJ	**1940**
Protein	**24** g
Fat	**4** g
CHO	**83** g

200 g/7 oz broccoli florets, divided into tiny sprigs

4 young carrots, thinly sliced

200 g/7 oz frozen petits pois

375 g/12 oz dried penne pasta

200 g/7 oz small button mushrooms, quartered

6 tablespoons dry white wine

2 tablespoons finely chopped parsley

300 ml/½ pint very low-fat natural yogurt

1 tablespoon grated Parmesan cheese

salt and pepper

1 Cook the broccoli and carrots in boiling salted water for 5–7 minutes until they are tender but still crunchy. Remove with a slotted spoon and drain. Add the petits pois to the water and bring back to the boil. Simmer for 3–4 minutes. Drain well.

2 Bring a large saucepan of salted water to the boil. Add the penne, stir and cook for 10–12 minutes until al dente.

3 Meanwhile, place the mushrooms, wine and parsley in a saucepan and season with salt and pepper. Cook for 8–10 minutes, stirring. Add the cooked vegetables and toss over a high heat to heat through.

4 Drain the penne thoroughly and turn into a warmed bowl. Add the low-fat yogurt and vegetables and toss quickly together. Divide the pasta equally among four warmed soup bowls. Sprinkle Parmesan on top and serve at once.

This recipe makes an ideal vegetarian supper dish. Serve with a crisp salad.

tagliatelle
sicilienne

4	Serves
10 minutes, plus standing	Preparation time
15–20 minutes	Cooking time
388	Kcal
1650	KJ
14 g	Protein
5 g	Fat
77 g	CHO

1 large aubergine, diced

1 tablespoon olive oil

2 onions, chopped

2 garlic cloves, chopped

400 g/13 oz can chopped plum
tomatoes

2 teaspoons chopped basil

375 g/12 oz fresh tagliatelle

salt and pepper

1 Sprinkle the diced aubergine with salt and leave for 30 minutes to remove any bitter taste. Rinse in cold water and dry well with kitchen paper.

2 Heat the oil in a saucepan, add the onions, garlic and aubergines and cook for 2–3 minutes. Add the tomatoes and their juice, together with the basil, and season to taste. Simmer for 15–20 minutes.

3 Meanwhile, bring a large pan of salted water to the boil. Put in the pasta, stir, and cook for 3–4 minutes until just al dente.

4 Drain the pasta, turn it into a warmed serving dish and top with the aubergine mixture.

If possible, use long, slim aubergines as these are drier and better for frying. Salting the aubergines draws out some of the moisture and possible bitterness, although some modern varieties do not need this treatment.

pasta twists
with bean sauce

Serves	**4**
Preparation time	**10** minutes
Cooking time	**20–25** minutes
Kcal	**460**
KJ	**1968**
Protein	**19** g
Fat	**4** g
CHO	**94** g

1 Heat a wok or heavy frying pan and dry fry the onion for 3–6 minutes, stirring constantly.

2 Add the pimentos and stir-fry for 1–2 minutes. Add the tomatoes with their juice, the beans and tomato purée and season to taste. Stir well, and simmer, for about 15 minutes.

1 small onion, finely chopped

185 g/6½ oz can pimentos (sweet red peppers), drained and thinly sliced

400 g/13 oz can chopped tomatoes with herbs

425 g/14 oz can mixed bean salad, drained

1 teaspoon tomato purée

375 g/12 oz dried wholewheat pasta twists or spirals

2 tablespoons chopped parsley

salt and pepper

chervil sprigs, to garnish

3 Meanwhile, bring a large saucepan of salted water to the boil. Add the pasta, stir and cook for 10–12 minutes until al dente.

4 Drain the pasta well and turn it into a warmed bowl. Stir half of the parsley into the bean sauce. Taste and adjust the seasoning, if necessary, and pour the sauce over the pasta, tossing well. Divide the pasta and its sauce equally among four warmed bowls. Scatter over the remaining parsley and serve at once, garnished with chervil sprigs.

Mixed bean salad is a combination of green, red kidney, black eye, borlotti and cannellini beans with chick peas, sweetcorn and red peppers.

stuffed peppers

4	Serves
10 minutes	Preparation time
about **1¼** hours	Cooking time
315	Kcal
1330	KJ
12 g	Protein
5 g	Fat
59 g	CHO

300 ml/½ pint water

175 g/6 oz brown rice

4 tomatoes, skinned and chopped

1 onion, grated

25 g/1 oz seedless raisins

75 g/3 oz low-fat Cheddar cheese, grated

2 tablespoons chopped parsley

pinch of ground cinnamon

4 red or green peppers, halved, cored and deseeded, with stalks left intact

5 tablespoons Vegetable Stock (see page 11)

salt and pepper

1 Bring the water to the boil with ½ teaspoon salt, add the rice and cook for 30 minutes, until the rice is tender and all the water has been absorbed.

2 When the rice is cooked, remove from the heat and gently stir in the tomatoes, onion and raisins. Stir in two-thirds of the cheese, then the parsley and cinnamon and season to taste with salt and pepper.

3 Arrange the pepper halves, cut side up, in an ovenproof dish. Divide the rice mixture equally among them and sprinkle the remaining cheese over the top. Pour the stock around the peppers and cover with foil. Bake in a preheated oven, 200°C (400° F), Gas Mark 6, for 30–40 minutes, or until tender.

Peppers can be stuffed with many different combinations of ingredients. Try adding chopped anchovies, cooked chicken or bacon to the filling.

tomato tagliatelle

Serves **6**

Preparation time about **20** minutes

Cooking time **15–20** minutes

Kcal **342**

KJ **1451**

Protein **13** g

Fat **4** g

CHO **68** g

1 tablespoon vegetable oil

2 onions, sliced

2 garlic cloves, crushed

500 g/1 lb courgettes, thinly sliced

1 green pepper, cored, deseeded
   and sliced

2 large tomatoes, skinned and
   chopped

250 g/8 oz button mushrooms,
   sliced

2 tablespoons chopped parsley

500 g/1 lb fresh tomato flavoured
   tagliatelle

salt and pepper

oregano sprigs, to garnish

1 To make the sauce, heat the oil in a saucepan and cook the onions gently for 3 minutes, stirring once or twice. Add the garlic, courgettes and green pepper and cook for 3 minutes. Add the tomatoes and mushrooms, stir well, cover the pan and simmer for 10 minutes, or until the vegetables are just tender. Season with salt and pepper and stir in the parsley.

2 Meanwhile, bring a large saucepan of lightly salted water to the boil. Add the pasta, stir and cook for about 5 minutes, or until al dente. Drain the pasta, rinse with hot water to stop it becoming sticky, and drain again. Return the pasta to the pan and keep warm.

3 Turn the tagliatelle into a warmed serving dish, pour on the sauce and toss well. Garnish with oregano sprigs and serve at once.

Fresh tomato tagliatelle is flavoured with tomato purée. It is an attractive pale orange colour.

spinach spaghetti

3	Serves
10 minutes	Preparation time
15 minutes	Cooking time
655	Kcal
2785	KJ
48 g	Protein
5 g	Fat
133 g	CHO

1 Bring a large saucepan of salted water to the boil. Add the pasta, stir and cook for 10–12 minutes until al dente.

2 Meanwhile, dry-fry the onion, turning constantly, until soft, but not browned. Add the spinach and cook for 2–3 minutes. Stir in the yogurt, quark, lemon juice, nutmeg and salt and pepper, and cook over a low heat without boiling. Drain the pasta and add to the hot spinach sauce; toss well then serve immediately.

250 g/8 oz dried spaghetti

1 onion, chopped

250 g/8 oz spinach, chopped

150 ml/¼ pint very low-fat natural yogurt

125 g/4 oz quark cheese

1 teaspoon lemon juice

¼ teaspoon grated nutmeg

salt and pepper

Fresh green spinach contains a high content of vitamins A and C, iron and folic acid. To save time, spinach can now be bought pre-prepared in packets.

pasta
with cauliflower

Serves	**4**
Preparation time	**10** minutes
Cooking time	about **15** minutes
Kcal	**463**
KJ	**1968**
Protein	**20** g
Fat	**5** g
CHO	**89** g

750 g/1½ lb cauliflower, divided into
  florets
425 g/14 oz mezze zite or macaroni
2 teaspoons olive oil
25 g/1 oz stale breadcrumbs
salt and pepper

1 Bring a large saucepan of salted water to the boil, add the cauliflower and cook for 3 minutes. Add the pasta and cook for 10–12 minutes until al dente.

2 Drain the cauliflower and pasta and pile into a warmed serving dish; keep hot. Heat the oil in a small saucepan, add the breadcrumbs and fry over a medium-high heat until well browned. Sprinkle over the cauliflower and pasta, season with pepper to taste and fold gently to mix. Serve immediately.

The breadcrumbs in this recipe are best when made from a 3–4 day old loaf of bread.

pasta
with rich tomato sauce

4	Serves
25 minutes	Preparation time
30 minutes	Cooking time
286	Kcal
1216	KJ
11 g	Protein
5 g	Fat
53 g	CHO

1 Put the onion and garlic into a saucepan with a little water and cook for about 7 minutes until soft but not browned. Add the tomatoes, tomato purée, sugar, marjoram and stock, and season with salt and pepper. Half cover the pan and simmer gently for 25 minutes.

1 large onion, sliced

1 garlic clove, crushed

750 g/1½ lb ripe tomatoes, skinned and chopped

1 tablespoon tomato purée

2 teaspoons sugar

2 tablespoons marjoram

150 ml/¼ pint Vegetable Stock (see page 11)

250 g/8 oz dried lasagne verde

salt and pepper

2 Remove the lid, increase the heat slightly and cook for 2–3 minutes to reduce the sauce – it should have a thick, rich consistency. Keep the sauce hot.

3 Meanwhile, bring a large saucepan of salted water to the boil, add the pasta, stir and cook for 10–12 minutes until al dente.

4 To make the crunchy topping, heat the low-fat spread in a pan, add the sunflower seeds and brown them, then stir in the breadcrumbs. Shake the pan over the heat until the breadcrumbs are browned.

5 Drain the pasta thoroughly, turn into a warmed serving dish, spoon the hot sauce over and top with the crunchy topping. Serve immediately.

crunchy topping:

15 g/½ oz low-fat spread

1 tablespoon sunflower seeds

25 g/1 oz wholemeal breadcrumbs

Sunflower seeds are the small, flat, oval seeds from the centre of the flowerhead of the sunflower plant. When toasted in a pan they become delicious and crunchy and give texture to this dish.

vegetable hot-pot

Serves **4**

Preparation time: **10** minutes

Cooking time: about **25** minutes

Kcal **166**

KJ **700**

Protein **6** g

Fat **2** g

CHO **32** g

4 carrots, sliced

4 parsnips, sliced

2 large courgettes, sliced

2 turnips, sliced

2 red or green peppers, cored, deseeded and coarsely chopped

2 onions, sliced

2 large tomatoes, peeled, deseeded and chopped

600 ml/1 pint Vegetable or Chicken Stock (see page 11)

1 bay leaf

1 tablespoon chopped parsley

1 teaspoon chopped thyme

1 teaspoon chopped marjoram

dash of Worcestershire sauce

salt and pepper

1 Place all the ingredients in a flameproof casserole. Bring to the boil, skim off any scum that rises to the surface, then cover and cook gently for about 25 minutes, until all the vegetables are tender. Serve the hotpot immediately.

Substitute or add vegetables of your choice to this hearty stew. Swede, leek and potato would be ideal.

penne
with aubergine

4	Serves
5 minutes, plus standing	Preparation time
30–35 minutes	Cooking time
260	Kcal
1110	KJ
10 g	Protein
2 g	Fat
54 g	CHO

1 Put the aubergine in a colander and sprinkle with salt. Leave for 30 minutes to remove any bitter taste, rinse and pat dry with kitchen paper.

2 Bring a large saucepan of salted water to the boil. Add the pasta, stir and cook for 10–12 minutes until al dente. Drain and keep warm.

3 Meanwhile, simmer the onion and garlic in a little water for 3–6 minutes, stirring constantly. Transfer into a shallow baking dish and place in a preheated oven, 180°C (350°F), Gas Mark 4, for about 6 minutes until soft. Return to a saucepan.

4 Add the aubergine to the saucepan and cook, stirring, until lightly browned. Stir in the mustard, tomato purée, tomatoes and their juice, herbs, salt and pepper to taste. Simmer gently for 10 minutes until the aubergine is cooked, stirring occasionally. Pour the sauce over the pasta and serve at once.

500 g/1 lb aubergine, cubed

250 g/8 oz dried penne pasta

1 onion, chopped

2 garlic cloves, crushed

1 teaspoon mustard powder

1 tablespoon tomato purée

400 g/13 oz can tomatoes

½ teaspoon dried oregano

1 tablespoon chopped parsley

salt and pepper

Be adventurous in selecting pasta shapes: rigatoni and mezze maniche are other short, tubular pasta types which would be suitable for this dish.

bean and pasta
curry

Serves	**4**
Preparation time	**20** minutes
Cooking time	**30** minutes
Kcal	**305**
KJ	**1293**
Protein	**13** g
Fat	**5** g
CHO	**56** g

150 g/5 oz pasta quills or twists

2 x 400 g/13 oz cans red kidney beans

parsley sprigs, to garnish

salt

sauce:

1 tablespoon vegetable oil

3 onions, chopped

2 garlic cloves, crushed

3 tablespoons curry powder

½ teaspoon ground cumin

½ teaspoon ground coriander

½ teaspoon chilli powder

2 teaspoons grated fresh root ginger (optional)

2 tablespoons wholemeal flour

900 ml/1½ pints Vegetable Stock (see page 11)

1 tablespoon lemon juice

1 To make the sauce, heat the oil in a saucepan with a lid and gently fry the onions and garlic for 2–3 minutes. Stir in the curry powder, cumin, coriander, chilli powder, ginger and flour and cook for 1 minute. Pour in the vegetable stock and lemon juice, bring to the boil, then cover and simmer gently for 25 minutes. Taste and add salt if necessary.

2 Meanwhile, bring a large saucepan of salted water to the boil. Add the pasta, stir and cook for 10–12 minutes until al dente. Drain and rinse. Drain the kidney beans, reserving the liquid for thinning the sauce.

3 Add the pasta and beans to the sauce, stirring them in gently. If the sauce is too thick, thin with the reserved bean liquid. Serve garnished with parsley sprigs.

Curry sauce improves with keeping and can be made the day before, and then simply reheated while the pasta cooks. Either way, a substantial meal can be made in about 30 minutes.

bucatini
del buongustaio

4	Serves
10 minutes	Preparation time
about **20–25** minutes	Cooking time
390	Kcal
1663	KJ
14 g	Protein
5 g	Fat
77 g	CHO

1 To make the sauce, heat the oil in a saucepan, add the onion, garlic and aubergine and cook for 5 minutes, then add the mushrooms and tomatoes, plus the juice from the can. Add the sage and a little salt and pepper. Cover the pan and cook gently for 15 minutes. Remove the sage.

250–375 g/8–12 oz bucatini

sauce:

1 tablespoon olive oil

1 large onion, finely chopped

2 garlic cloves, finely chopped

1 aubergine, peeled and diced

125 g/4 oz mushrooms, sliced

400 g/13 oz can chopped plum
   tomatoes

1 sage sprig

salt and pepper

2 Meanwhile, bring a large saucepan of salted water to the boil. Add the pasta, stir and cook for 10–12 minutes until al dente. Drain the pasta well and add to the sauce.

3 Heat the pasta with the sauce for 1 minute, stirring gently to blend the two together, then serve at once.

Bucatini is a long pasta, not unlike spaghetti, which could be substituted if you prefer.

pasta
syracuse style

Serves	**6**
Preparation time	**15** minutes
Cooking time	about **30** minutes
Kcal	**345**
KJ	**1464**
Protein	**13** g
Fat	**4** g
CHO	**69** g

1 Heat a large frying pan or wok and dry-fry the onion and garlic for 3–6 minutes, turning constantly, until soft. Add the courgettes and cook for 10 minutes. Add the green pepper, tomatoes, olives, anchovies, parsley, marjoram and salt and pepper to taste. Bring to the boil, stirring. Cover the pan and simmer while cooking the pasta.

1 large onion, sliced

2 garlic cloves, crushed

500 g/1 lb courgettes, chopped

1 green pepper, cored, deseeded and chopped

400 g/13 oz can tomatoes, drained and roughly chopped

125 g/4 oz black olives, pitted

3 anchovy fillets, finely chopped

1 tablespoon chopped parsley

2 teaspoons chopped marjoram

500 g/1 lb dried fettucine

salt and pepper

flat leaf parsley sprigs, to garnish

2 Meanwhile, bring a large saucepan of salted water to the boil. Add the pasta, stir and cook for 10–12 minutes until al dente. Drain well and place in a warmed serving dish. Add the sauce and toss lightly together. Garnish with the parsley and serve at once.

Use long, flat, ribbon-shaped pasta such as tagliatelle, linguine or tagliarini instead of the fettucine, if liked.

pasta bows
with tomatoes and mushrooms

2	Serves
10 minutes	Preparation time
25 minutes	Cooking time
364	Kcal
1548	KJ
14 g	Protein
4 g	Fat
74 g	CHO

1 Bring a large saucepan of salted water to the boil. Add the pasta, stir and cook for 10–12 minutes until al dente. Drain and keep warm.

2 Meanwhile, make the sauce. Heat the oil in a saucepan, add the sliced onion and mushrooms and sauté for 5 minutes. Stir in the tomatoes and cook gently, uncovered, for 15 minutes to reduce the sauce. Add the basil and simmer for a further 5 minutes. Season to taste, pour over the pasta bows and serve.

175 g/6 oz dried tri-colour pasta bows

sauce:
1 teaspoon sunflower oil

1 small onion, finely chopped

125 g/4 oz mushrooms, sliced

400 g/13 oz can tomatoes

1 tablespoon chopped basil

salt and pepper

This simple colourful dish is ideal for children, who really enjoy it as it is made with tri-coloured pasta (plain, spinach and tomato-flavoured).

spaghetti
peperonata

Serves	**4**
Preparation time	**15** minutes
Cooking time	**25** minutes
Kcal	**370**
KJ	**1575**
Protein	**14** g
Fat	**2** g
CHO	**79** g

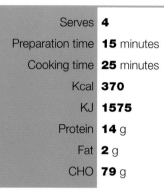

300–375 g/10–12 oz dried spaghetti

sauce:

2 tablespoons olive oil

3 onions, finely chopped

2 garlic cloves, finely chopped

400 g/13 oz can chopped plum
   tomatoes

1 tablespoon tomato purée

1 tablespoon chopped oregano

2 bay leaves

1 green pepper, cored, deseeded
   and diced

1 red pepper, cored, deseeded and
   diced

salt and pepper

1 First make the sauce. Heat the oil in a saucepan and add the onion and garlic and cook for 5 minutes.

2 Add the tomatoes with their juice, the tomato purée, oregano, bay leaves and salt and pepper to taste. Simmer for 10 minutes, then add the diced red and green peppers. Cook for 10 minutes, or until the peppers are just soft. Remove the bay leaves before serving.

3 Meanwhile, bring a large saucepan of salted water to the boil. Add the spaghetti, stir and cook for 10–12 minutes until al dente.

4 Drain the pasta thoroughly, rinse with hot water and drain again. Pile on to a warmed dish or individual plates. Top with the sauce and serve immediately.

This delicious spaghetti has a fresh, spicy flavour and is perfect for a winter's lunch or supper.

pasta
with ratatouille sauce

4	Serves
15–20 minutes	Preparation time
35 minutes	Cooking time
509	Kcal
2168	KJ
19 g	Protein
4 g	Fat
107 g	CHO

1 Put all the ingredients, except the pasta and parsley, into a large saucepan. Add enough water to cover the vegetables and cook gently, stirring occasionally, for 30 minutes until the vegetables are tender and the juices have thickened slightly.

2 Meanwhile, bring a large saucepan of salted water to the boil. Add the pasta, stir and cook for 10–12 minutes until just al dente. Drain and place in a warmed serving dish.

3 Taste the sauce and adjust the seasoning if necessary, then pour over the pasta. Garnish with the parsley and serve hot.

1 large onion, chopped

1 garlic clove, crushed

500 g/1 lb courgettes, sliced

1 large aubergine, diced

1 green pepper, cored, deseeded
   and diced

500 g/1 lb tomatoes, skinned and
   chopped

1 tablespoon chopped oregano or
   basil

500 g/1 lb dried spaghetti

salt and pepper

1 tablespoon chopped parsley, to
   garnish

This sauce can be served cold as a starter, without the pasta.

spaghetti
with garlic and chilli

Serves	**6**
Preparation time	**10** minutes
Cooking time	about **12** minutes
Kcal	**320**
KJ	**1354**
Protein	**10** g
Fat	**5** g
CHO	**62** g

2 tablespoons olive oil

4 garlic cloves, finely chopped

1 red chilli, deseeded and chopped

500 g/1 lb dried spaghetti

2 tablespoons chopped parsley

salt and pepper

1 Heat the oil in a saucepan, add the garlic and chilli and fry gently for 1–2 minutes.

2 Bring a large saucepan of salted water to the boil. Add the pasta, stir and cook for 10–12 minutes until al dente. Drain and toss with the garlic mixture and the parsley. Season with black pepper and serve immediately.

This simple supper dish takes a matter of minutes to prepare, yet is full of flavour.

linguine
al pomodoro

6	Serves
15 minutes	Preparation time
45 minutes	Cooking time
344	Kcal
1463	KJ
12 g	Protein
4 g	Fat
69 g	CHO

1 tablespoon olive oil

2 celery sticks, finely chopped

1 large carrot, finely chopped

1 small onion, finely chopped

2 garlic cloves, crushed

1 kg/2 lb ripe plum tomatoes,
   roughly chopped

1 teaspoon caster sugar

2 tablespoons chopped basil

500 g/1 lb dried linguine

salt and pepper

torn basil leaves, to garnish

grated Parmesan cheese, to serve

1 Heat the oil in a saucepan, add the celery, carrot, onion and garlic and fry gently for 5 minutes until softened.

2 Stir in the tomatoes, sugar and basil, and season to taste with salt and pepper. Bring to the boil, cover and simmer gently for 30 minutes.

3 Transfer the sauce to a food processor or blender and purée. Rub the purée through a sieve.

4 Bring a large saucepan of salted water to the boil. Add the pasta, stir and cook for 10–12 minutes until al dente. Drain and toss with the sauce. Transfer to a serving dish, garnish with torn basil leaves and serve immediately with a little Parmesan.

The combination of tomatoes and basil is heavenly. A little sugar is added to sweeten the tomatoes. Leave it out if they are already sweet and ripe.

broccoli sauce
with chilli and conchiglie

Serves	**6**
Preparation time	**10** minutes
Cooking time	about **15** minutes
Kcal	**329**
KJ	**1395**
Protein	**14** g
Fat	**4** g
CHO	**63** g

500 g/1 lb broccoli florets

500 g/1 lb dried conchiglie

dried chilli flakes, to taste

25 g/1 oz low-fat spread

salt and pepper

1 Put the broccoli florets into a large pan of lightly salted boiling water and cook for 3 minutes until just tender. Drain and break into smaller pieces. Dice the stalks.

2 Bring a large saucepan of salted water to the boil. Add the pasta, stir and cook for 10–12 minutes until al dente. Drain and transfer to a warmed serving dish, reserving a little of the pasta water.

3 Add the broccoli, chilli flakes and low-fat spread. Season to taste with salt and pepper. Toss well before serving, adding a little pasta water, if necessary, to keep the mixture moist.

Substitute the broccoli with cauliflower, fennel strips or courgette slices, if liked.

spaghetti
with mushrooms and herbs

2	Serves
8–10 minutes	Preparation time
about **12** minutes	Cooking time
404	Kcal
1715	KJ
14 g	Protein
5 g	Fat
78 g	CHO

1 Bring a large saucepan of salted water to the boil. Add the pasta, stir and cook for 10–12 minutes until al dente.

2 Meanwhile, heat the oil in a saucepan, add the onion and garlic and fry gently for 2–3 minutes.

200 g/7 oz dried spaghetti

2 teaspoons olive oil

75 g/3 oz onion, finely sliced

1 garlic clove, crushed

175 g/6 oz mushrooms, finely
  sliced

1 tablespoon fresh mixed herbs

1 teaspoon dried sage, oregano or
  thyme

2 tablespoons white wine

salt and pepper

3 Add the mushrooms, then the herbs and season with salt and pepper. Continue to fry gently for a few minutes until the mushrooms have softened and darkened, add the white wine and simmer for about 5 minutes.

4 Drain the pasta and pile into a warmed serving dish. Toss with the sauce and serve immediately.

This is a simple, easy-to-cook lunch or supper dish.

corsican cannelloni

Serves	**4**
Preparation time	**15** minutes
Cooking time	**50** minutes
Kcal	**435**
KJ	**1848**
Protein	**20** g
Fat	**5** g
CHO	**83** g

750 ml/1¼ pints boiling water

½ teaspoon vegetable oil

8 sheets no-need-to-precook
  lasagne verde

425 g/14 oz can ratatouille

125 g/4 oz frozen broad beans

2 teaspoons chopped mixed herbs

400 g/13 oz can chopped tomatoes

pepper

50 g/2 oz low-fat Cheddar cheese,
  grated, to serve

1 Pour the boiling water into a large, shallow, ovenproof dish and add the oil. Slide the sheets of lasagne into the dish and leave them for a few minutes to soften.

2 Put the ratatouille and beans into a saucepan and cook for about 10 minutes, or until the beans are soft. Drain well. Add the herbs and pepper to taste.

3 Remove the lasagne sheets and drain, then spread them on a clean work surface. Divide the vegetable filling among the lasagne sheets, then roll them up to make cannelloni.

4 Place the cannelloni in a shallow ovenproof dish and spoon over the chopped tomatoes. Cook in a preheated oven, 180°C (350°F), Gas Mark 4, for 30 minutes.

5 To serve, sprinkle the cannelloni with the grated cheese and place under a preheated grill until browned.

Use no-need-to-precook cannelloni instead, if liked. Fill the dry tubes, then bake until tender, as in the recipe.

rigatoni
with courgette sauce

4	Serves
15 minutes	Preparation time
15–20 minutes	Cooking time
414	kcal
1758	kJ
16 g	Protein
5 g	Fat
82 g	CHO

2 teaspoons olive oil

2 onions, finely chopped

8 courgettes, thinly sliced

500 g/1 lb rigatoni

1 tablespoon grated Parmesan

   cheese

salt

1 First make the sauce. Heat the oil in a large frying pan, add the onions and fry gently for about 5 minutes until soft and transparent. Add the courgettes and fry them gently until just tender, stiring frequently to prevent them sticking. Cover the pan if the courgettes start to burn on the outside before being cooked through. Add salt to taste.

2 Meanwhile, bring a large saucepan of salted water to the boil. Add the rigatoni, stir and cook for 10–12 minutes until al dente. Drain the pasta, reserving a small quantity of the cooking water. Transfer the rigatoni to a warmed serving dish and mix in the courgettes and onions, adding a ladleful of the cooking water and the Parmesan to form a moist, creamy mixture. Serve immediately with a little extra Parmesan, if liked.

If any courgette flowers are available, they can be washed, sliced and added to the courgettes and onions while frying. The flowers have a very delicate flavour.

spaghetti
with lentil bolognese sauce

Serves	**4**
Preparation time	**1** hour
Cooking time	**45** minutes
Kcal	**439**
KJ	**1864**
Protein	**18** g
Fat	**5** g
CHO	**85** g

250 g/8 oz whole green lentils

2 teaspoons vegetable oil

2 onions, chopped

2 garlic cloves, crushed

2 celery sticks, chopped

2 carrots, finely diced

2 tablespoons tomato purée

375 g/12 oz dried spaghetti

15 g/½ oz low-fat spread

salt and pepper

1 To make the sauce, rinse the lentils, place in a pan, cover with water and bring to the boil. Simmer gently for about 40 minutes until tender. Drain, reserving the liquid.

2 Heat the oil in a large saucepan, add the onions and cook for 5 minutes until soft, then add the garlic, celery and carrots. Cook the vegetables, covered, for 15 minutes, until tender.

3 Stir in the lentils, tomato purée, salt and pepper and a little of the reserved lentil cooking liquid to make a thick, soft consistency. Simmer the sauce for about 10 minutes, adding more liquid if necessary.

4 Bring a large saucepan of salted water to the boil. Add the spaghetti, stir and cook for 10–12 minutes until al dente. Drain the spaghetti, then return to the saucepan with the low-fat spread and season with pepper. Make sure the spaghetti is hot, then turn it on to a hot serving plate and pour the sauce on top.

Unlike some types of lentils, green lentils do not need lengthy pre-soaking. Simply rinse, then cook.

spaghetti
with three herb sauce

4	Serves
15 minutes	Preparation time
10–12 minutes	Cooking time
317	Kcal
1343	KJ
12 g	Protein
5 g	Fat
58 g	CHO

3 tablespoons chopped parsley

1 tablespoon chopped tarragon

2 tablespoons chopped basil

1 tablespoon olive oil

1 large garlic clove, crushed

4 tablespoons Vegetable or Chicken
  Stock (see page 11)

2 tablespoons dry white wine

375 g/12 oz dried multi-coloured
  spaghetti

salt and pepper

1 Put the parsley, tarragon, basil, olive oil, garlic, stock, white wine and salt and pepper to taste into a food processor or blender and work until smooth.

2 Cook the spaghetti in a large pan of boiling salted water for 10–12 minutes until just tender.

3 Drain the spaghetti and heap in a warmed bowl; pour over the herb sauce and toss well, then serve immediately.

Parsley, tarragon and basil combine well together, but many other combinations of herbs would work: experiment with whatever herbs you have to hand.

chinese-style
vermicelli

Serves	**4**
Preparation time	**15** minutes
Cooking time	**20** minutes
Kcal	**320**
KJ	**1336**
Protein	**9** g
Fat	**5** g
CHO	**61** g

250 g/8 oz dried vermicelli

4 carrots, cut into fine matchsticks

4 courgettes, cut into fine
 matchsticks

125 g/4 oz small mangetout

5 teaspoons oil

4 spring onions, sliced diagonally

2.5 cm/1 inch piece of fresh root
 ginger, peeled and sliced into
 matchsticks

1–2 garlic cloves, crushed

4 tablespoons light soy sauce

1 tablespoon clear honey

1 tablespoon white wine vinegar

1 teaspoon coriander seeds,
 crushed

salt and pepper

parsley leaves, to garnish

1 Bring a large saucepan of salted water to the boil. Add the vermicelli, stir and bring back to the boil. Reduce the heat slightly and boil, uncovered, for 8–10 minutes, or until al dente, stirring occasionally.

2 Meanwhile, put the carrots, courgettes and mangetout into a colander or sieve and place over the pan of boiling vermicelli. Cover the colander and steam the vegetables for about 5 minutes until they are tender but still crunchy. Remove the colander and set it aside. Drain the vermicelli when it is still al dente.

3 Heat the oil in a wok or deep frying pan. Add the spring onions and ginger and cook gently, stirring, until the ingredients give off a spicy aroma. Add the garlic, soy sauce, honey, wine vinegar and coriander seeds, stirring well. Add the vermicelli and vegetables. Increase the heat and vigorously toss the ingredients in the wok until they are evenly combined and very hot. Season with salt and pepper to taste. Turn into a warmed serving bowl and garnish with parsley leaves. Serve at once.

peperonata
with wholewheat noodles

6	Serves
20–25 minutes	Preparation time
20 minutes	Cooking time
170	Kcal
720	KJ
6 g	Protein
5 g	Fat
28 g	CHO

2 tablespoons olive oil

1 large onion, thinly sliced

1 large garlic clove, crushed

2 red peppers, cored, deseeded and
   cut into strips

2 green peppers, cored, deseeded
   and cut into strips

375 g/12 oz tomatoes, skinned,
   deseeded and chopped

1 tablespoon chopped basil

175 g/6 oz wholewheat noodles

salt and pepper

basil sprigs, to garnish

1 Heat 1 tablespoon of the olive oil in a deep frying pan. Add the onion and garlic and cook very gently until the onion is soft but not coloured. Add the peppers, tomatoes, basil and salt and pepper to taste. Cover and cook gently for 10 minutes.

2 Remove the lid from the pan and cook over fairly high heat until most of the moisture has evaporated. Keep the vegetable mixture warm.

3 Meanwhile, cook the noodles in plenty of boiling salted water until just tender. Drain the noodles thoroughly and toss in the remaining olive oil. Add salt and pepper to taste.

4 Divide the noodles among 4 serving plates and spoon the hot peperonata over the top. Garnish with sprigs of fresh basil and serve immediately, as a light main course with a salad.

Peperonata is a classic summer dish, combining the best of summer produce – peppers, fresh tomatoes and fresh basil. Use fresh wholewheat noodles if you can – these take about 8–10 minutes to cook, but the extra time is well worth it for the flavour.

salads

The salads in this chapter combine contrasting colours and textures with low-fat dressings. Some make a meal in themselves, while others are interesting side dishes.

and side dishes

tagliatelle salad

Serves **6**

Preparation time **15** minutes

Cooking time **5** minutes

Kcal **500**

KJ **2129**

Protein **39** g

Fat **4** g

CHO **84** g

500 g/1 lb fresh tagliatelle verde

2 x 425 g/14 oz cans red kidney
    beans, rinsed and drained

2 x 200 g/7 oz cans tuna in brine,
    drained and flaked

4 courgettes, thinly sliced

50 g/2 oz mushrooms, thinly sliced

2 shallots, chopped

1 tablespoon green peppercorns

1 Bring a large saucepan of salted water to the boil. Add the pasta, stir and cook for 4–5 minutes until al dente. Drain and cool quickly under cold running water. Drain thoroughly and place in a large bowl.

2 Add the kidney beans, tuna, courgettes, mushrooms and shallots to the pasta along with the peppercorns. Mix together well.

dressing:

4 tablespoons low-fat natural
    yogurt

2 tablespoons chopped parsley

2 tablespoons chopped chives

2 teaspoons lemon juice

1 teaspoon finely grated lemon rind

cayenne pepper

salt

to garnish:

mint sprigs (optional)

lemon wedges

3 Mix all the dressing ingredients together, and season with cayenne pepper and salt to taste. Fold the dressing into the salad and transfer to a large serving bowl.

4 Garnish with mint sprigs, if using, and lemon wedges. Serve immediately.

Serve this salad with fresh crusty bread to mop up the dressing.

pasta, cucumber
and radish salad

4	Serves
25 minutes	Preparation time
about **12** minutes	Cooking time
149	Kcal
630	KJ
7 g	Protein
1 g	Fat
29 g	CHO

1 Bring a large saucepan of salted water to the boil. Add the pasta, stir and cook for 10–12 minutes until al dente. Rinse under cold running water and drain thoroughly.

2 Put the radishes and cucumber into a bowl and add the pasta.

125 g/4 oz dried pasta shapes

175 g/6 oz radishes, sliced

½ cucumber, diced

150 ml/¼ pint low-fat yogurt

1 Cos lettuce

salt and pepper

2 finely chopped spring onions, to garnish

3 Stir in the yogurt, season with plenty of pepper and a little salt. Toss the pasta, radishes and cucumber in the yogurt to coat thoroughly.

4 Arrange the lettuce leaves on a serving dish and spoon the salad into them. Garnish with the chopped spring onions.

Any other crisp lettuce, such as romaine or little gem, would also be good in this salad.

celeriac
and carrot remoulade

Serves	**4** as a side salad
Preparation time	**20** minutes
Cooking time	**10** minutes
Kcal	**94**
KJ	**390**
Protein	**4** g
Fat	**4** g
CHO	**11** g

1 Drop the celeriac strips as you cut them into a bowl of water with 1 tablespoon of the lemon juice.

2 Partly cook the celeriac and carrot strips for 5–8 minutes in boiling salted water with the remaining lemon juice. Drain, dry on kitchen paper and leave to cool.

3 To make the dressing, mix the ingredients in a bowl. Taste and adjust the seasoning if necessary.

4 Toss the celeriac and carrots in the dressing and spoon the salad on to a serving dish. Garnish with the hard-boiled egg and chives and serve.

1 celeriac root, about 250 g/8 oz, sliced into matchstick strips

2 tablespoons lemon juice

250 g/8 oz carrots, sliced into matchstick strips

salt

dressing:

4 tablespoons low-fat mayonnaise

150 ml/¼ pint very low-fat natural yogurt

1 garlic clove, crushed

1 tablespoon chopped parsley

1 tablespoon finely snipped chives

½ teaspoon mustard powder

pinch of cayenne pepper

to garnish:

1 hard-boiled egg, chopped

snipped chives

Celeriac is a root vegetable which resembles a large, knobbly turnip. It has a sweet, nutty celery flavour.

scalloped
potatoes

6	Serves
20 minutes	Preparation time
1 hour **20** minutes	Cooking time
185	Kcal
777	KJ
5 g	Protein
5 g	Fat
30 g	CHO

2 teaspoons vegetable oil

75 ml/3 fl oz low-fat soured cream

350 ml/12 fl oz skimmed milk

25 g/1 oz low-fat spread

1 tablespoon cornflour

⅛ teaspoon pepper

**750 g/1½ lb large potatoes, cut into
5 mm/¼ inch slices**

½ onion, diced

to garnish:

paprika

thyme sprigs

1 Brush a large, shallow, rectangular baking dish with oil.

2 In a medium bowl, whisk together the soured cream, skimmed milk, low-fat spread, cornflour and pepper.

3 Line the dish with one-third of the potato slices. Pour one-third of the soured cream mixture over the potatoes. Sprinkle half of the onion over the soured cream mixture. Repeat the layers in order: one-third of the potatoes, one-third of the soured cream mixture and the remaining onion. Arrange the remaining potatoes on the top and pour the remaining soured cream mixture over the top. Cover with foil and bake in a preheated oven, 180°C (350°F), Gas Mark 4, for 1 hour. Remove the foil and bake for a further 20 minutes.

4 Sprinkle with paprika and thyme sprigs, then leave to stand for 5 minutes before serving.

This makes a wonderful accompaniment to grilled meat or poultry. Serve with a green vegetable.

honey carrots

Serves **6**

Preparation time **10** minutes

Cooking time **12** minutes

Kcal **87**

KJ **365**

Protein **1** g

Fat **3** g

CHO **16** g

750 g/1½ lb baby carrots

1 tablespoon margarine

½ tablespoon soft light brown sugar

2 tablespoons honey

2–3 tablespoons finely chopped

   fresh parsley

1 Bring a large saucepan of water to the boil, add the carrots, reduce the heat, cover and simmer for about 10 minutes, or until the carrots are tender-crisp. Drain and set aside.

2 Melt the margarine in a frying pan over a medium-high heat. Add the sugar, honey and carrots. Reduce the heat and turn the carrots frequently for 1–2 minutes until well glazed. Sprinkle with parsley before serving.

Baby carrots are harvested young so they are sweet and full of flavour.

herring
and apple salad

4	Serves
10 minutes	Preparation time
about **12** minutes	Cooking time
248	Kcal
1049	KJ
13 g	Protein
5 g	Fat
40 g	CHO

125 g/4 oz large dried pasta shells

150 g/5 oz low-fat natural yogurt

2 tablespoons raisins

2 red dessert apples, cored and
thinly sliced

grated rind and juice of ½ lemon

1 tablespoon chopped parsley

2 small rollmops, cut into pieces

salt and pepper

1 Bring a large saucepan of salted water to the boil. Add the pasta, stir and cook for 10–12 minutes until al dente. Rinse and drain. While warm, mix the pasta with a little diluted yogurt and stir in the raisins and apples.

2 Mix the remaining yogurt with the lemon rind and juice, and the parsley and season to taste.

3 Place the pasta on a shallow serving dish and arrange the rollmops on top. Spoon over the sauce and serve.

Rollmops are herring fillets which are rolled up with onions, gherkins and peppercorns and marinated in vinegar. They are usually sold in jars.

pasta slaw

Serves **4**

Preparation time **15** minutes

Cooking time **10–12** minutes

Kcal **146**

KJ **612**

Protein **5** g

Fat **5** g

CHO **22** g

75 g/3 oz dried fusilli pasta

300 g/10 oz French beans

75 g/3 oz white cabbage, roughly
   chopped

1 carrot, grated

4 spring onions, finely chopped

salt and pepper

parsley sprigs, to garnish (optional)

dressing:

4 tablespoons low-fat mayonnaise

2 tablespoons skimmed milk

1 tablespoon balsamic or wine
   vinegar

2 teaspoons sugar

salt and pepper

1 Bring a saucepan of salted water to the boil. Add the pasta, stir and cook for 10–12 minutes until al dente. At the same time, bring a second pan of salted water to the boil and cook the French beans for 3–5 minutes. Refresh the pasta and beans under cold running water, drain and leave to cool.

2 Meanwhile, mix together the remaining salad ingredients in a bowl. Combine the ingredients for the dressing in a jug and add to the salad bowl with the pasta and French beans. Season to taste and garnish with parsley sprigs, if using, and serve.

Balsamic vinegar is dark and mellow with a sweet-sour flavour. It is made around Modena in Italy.

fennel
and pasta salad

4	Serves
15 minutes	Preparation time
10–12 minutes	Cooking time
497	Kcal
2114	KJ
17 g	Protein
5 g	Fat
103 g	CHO

500 g/1 lb dried conchiglie or farfalle pasta

3 large fennel bulbs, sliced, leaves reserved for garnish

2–3 red dessert apples, cored and sliced

juice of 1 lemon

4 shallots, chopped

4 tomatoes, skinned and chopped

dressing:

3 teaspoons olive oil

2 tablespoons lemon juice

1 teaspoon French mustard

1 teaspoon honey

1 tablespoon each chopped parsley and basil

1 Bring a large saucepan of salted water to the boil. Add the pasta, stir and cook for 10–12 minutes until al dente. Drain and cool quickly under cold running water. Drain thoroughly and place in a large bowl.

2 Toss the fennel and apples in the lemon juice, then add to the pasta with the shallots and tomatoes.

3 Mix the dressing ingredients together and pour over the salad. Transfer to a serving bowl and garnish with the reserved fennel leaves. Serve immediately.

Fennel brings an unusual sweet aniseed flavour and special crispness to this pasta salad.

caponata

Serves **6**

Preparation time **20** minutes

Cooking time **1** hour **20** minutes

Kcal **74**

KJ **313**

Protein **3** g

Fat **4** g

CHO **7** g

2 tablespoons olive oil

1 onion, thinly sliced

2 celery sticks, diced

3 aubergines cut into 1 cm/½ inch
   dice

150 ml/¼ pint passata

3 tablespoons wine vinegar

1 yellow pepper, cored, deseeded
   and thinly sliced

1 red pepper, cored, deseeded and
   thinly sliced

25 g/1 oz anchovy fillets, soaked in
   warm water, drained and dried

50 g/2 oz capers, roughly chopped

25 g/1 oz black olives, pitted and
   sliced

25 g/1 oz green olives, pitted and
   sliced

2 tablespoons chopped parsley, to
   serve

1 Heat the oil in a saucepan, add the onion and sauté until soft and golden. Add the celery and cook for 2–3 minutes. Add the aubergine and cook gently for 3 minutes, stirring occasionally.

2 Add the passata and cook gently until it has been absorbed. Add the wine vinegar and cook for 1 minute. Add the peppers, anchovies, capers and olives and cook for 3 minutes.

3 Transfer the mixture to an ovenproof dish and bake, covered, in a preheated oven, 180°C (350°F), Gas Mark 4, for about 1 hour. Serve lukewarm or cold sprinkled with chopped parsley.

This aubergine dish originated in Sicily. Serve on its own with crusty bread as a light meal, or as an accompaniment to plain grilled fish or chicken.

smoked chicken
and fruit salad

8	Serves
25 minutes	Preparation time
116	Kcal
485	KJ
11 g	Protein
5 g	Fat
6 g	CHO

1 lettuce, shredded

2 celery sticks, chopped

1 red pepper, cored, deseeded and
 sliced

25 g/1 oz walnut halves

75 g/3 oz green grapes, peeled,
 halved and deseeded

1 pear, peeled, cored and sliced

250 g/8 oz smoked chicken,
 skinned, boned and cut into strips

dressing:

2 tablespoons low-fat natural
 yogurt

2 tablespoons low-fat mayonnaise

2 tablespoons grated cucumber

1 teaspoon grated onion

½ teaspoon chopped tarragon

salt and pepper

to garnish:

1 pear, cored and sliced

tarragon sprigs

1 In a large salad bowl, mix the lettuce with the celery, red pepper, walnuts, grapes, pear and smoked chicken.

2 Mix the yogurt with the mayonnaise, cucumber, onion and tarragon, blending well. Add salt and pepper to taste.

3 Just before serving, spoon the dressing over the salad ingredients and toss well to mix.

4 Garnish with slices of pear and a few sprigs of fresh tarragon.

Any leftover smoked chicken will keep well and can be used in sandwiches. Use the bones to flavour stock.

chicory, orange
and pasta salad

Serves	**4**
Preparation time	**15** minutes
Cooking time	about **5** minutes
Kcal	**540**
KJ	**2298**
Protein	**18** g
Fat	**5** g
CHO	**114** g

500 g/1 lb fresh tagliatelle, cut into

   short lengths

4 heads of chicory, sliced

6 large oranges, peeled and

   segmented

2 tablespoons chopped tarragon

4 tablespoons chopped chives

dressing:

3 teaspoons olive oil

2 tablespoons orange juice

2 tablespoons lemon juice

½ teaspoon coarse-grain mustard

1 teaspoon honey

1 teaspoon mixed herbs

1 teaspoon finely grated orange

   rind

1 Bring a large saucepan of salted water to the boil. Add the pasta, stir and cook for 4–5 minutes until al dente. Drain and cool quickly under cold running water. Drain thoroughly and place in a large bowl.

2 Mix together the dressing ingredients and pour over the pasta.

3 Stir in the chicory, orange segments and herbs. Transfer to a serving dish and serve immediately.

Chicory has a bitter flavour which is complemented by the sweet dressing. Choose crisp, firm white heads.

duck salad
with mango

6	Serves
25 minutes	Preparation time
20 minutes	Cooking time
386	Kcal
1640	KJ
16 g	Protein
5 g	Fat
72 g	CHO

1 Arrange the duck breasts, skin-side up, on a rack and roast in a preheated oven for 10 minutes on each side.

3 boneless duck breasts, about
175 g/6 oz each

1 bunch of spring onions, cut into
2.5 cm/1 inch lengths

1 celery stick, chopped

1 teaspoon grated orange rind

500 g/1 lb brown rice, cooked

3 medium ripe mangoes, peeled
and sliced

salt and pepper

2 Leave to cool, then remove the skin and cube the meat.

3 Meanwhile, make the sauce. Place the egg white, whole egg, mustard, mango chutney, soy sauce and vinegar in a food processor or blender and blend well, then add the yogurt, a tablespoon at a time.

4 Combine the duck meat with the onions, celery, orange rind, cooked rice and seasoning in a large bowl.

sauce:

1 egg white

1 whole egg

1 teaspoon Dijon mustard

1 tablespoon mango chutney

½ tablespoon soy sauce

1 tablespoon light vinegar,
preferably a fruit vinegar

250 ml/8 fl oz very low-fat natural
yogurt

5 Arrange the mango slices on top of the salad and serve, accompanied by the sauce.

Try to use Barbary duck breasts as they are less fatty than other duck breasts. The skin is thin and does not have a layer of fat underneath.

pasta twist salad

Serves **6**

Preparation time **15** minutes, plus chilling

Cooking time about **30** minutes

Kcal **134**

KJ **571**

Protein **5** g

Fat **1** g

CHO **28** g

125 g/4 oz dried wholewheat fusilli pasta

175 g/6 oz frozen sweetcorn kernels

4 celery sticks, sliced

4 tomatoes, skinned, quartered and seeded

4 spring onions, chopped

dressing:

150 g/5 oz low-fat natural yogurt

4 tablespoons tomato juice

¼ teaspoon Worcestershire sauce

2 teaspoons chopped oregano (optional)

pinch of sugar

salt and pepper

to garnish:

1 tablespoon parsley

celery leaves

1 Bring a large saucepan of salted water to the boil. Add the pasta, stir and cook for 12–14 minutes until al dente. Drain and rinse under cold running water.

2 Meanwhile, cook the sweetcorn until tender in a saucepan of boiling water, following the packet instructions. Drain and leave to cool.

3 Mix together the pasta and sweetcorn with the celery, tomatoes and spring onions in a bowl.

4 Blend together all the dressing ingredients in a jug, then pour the dressing over the salad and toss well.

5 Spoon the salad into a serving dish and sprinkle with parsley. Cover and chill for about 30 minutes before serving garnished with celery leaves.

Wholewheat pasta is made using the whole wheat grain, so it provides more protein, fibre and vitamins.

wholewheat
pasta salad

4	Serves
10–12 minutes, plus chilling	Preparation time
12 minutes	Cooking time
245	Kcal
1040	KJ
10 g	Protein
3 g	Fat
47 g	CHO

250 g/8 oz dried plain or
wholewheat fusilli pasta

100 ml/3½ fl oz fresh orange juice

2 tablespoons fresh lime juice

1 tablespoon fresh lemon juice

1 teaspoon cider vinegar

½ teaspoon granular low-calorie
sweetener

2 spring onions, chopped

125 g/4 oz French beans, cooked

4 tomatoes, skinned, quartered and
deseeded

salt and pepper

50 g/2 oz pitted black olives, to
garnish

1 Bring a large saucepan of salted water to the boil. Add the pasta, stir and cook for 12–14 minutes until al dente. Drain well.

2 Mix together the fresh orange, lime and lemon juices, the cider vinegar and the sweetener in a bowl. Season generously with pepper and pour over the hot pasta. Mix well together, cover and leave until cold.

3 Stir the spring onions, beans and tomatoes into the pasta and mix well with the dressing. To serve, turn into a large salad bowl and scatter over the black olives.

For the best flavour, buy olives loose in good delicatessens, or from the delicatessen counter in a supermarket. Green olives or stuffed olives could be used instead of black ones.

mushroom,
courgette and tomato salad

Serves	**4**
Preparation time	**10** minutes
Kcal	**25**
KJ	**107**
Protein	**2** g
Fat	**0** g
CHO	**4** g

6 large mushrooms, sliced

4 courgettes, thinly sliced

4 tomatoes, skinned and quartered

1 teaspoon chopped basil

1 bunch of cress, trimmed and
    divided into strips

Citrus Dressing (see below), to
    serve

citrus dressing:

100 ml/3½ fl oz fresh orange juice

2 tablespoons lime juice

1 tablespoon lemon juice

1 teaspoon cider vinegar

½ teaspoon granular low-calorie
    sweetener

pepper

1 Combine the mushrooms, courgettes and tomatoes in a salad bowl and sprinkle with the chopped basil.

2 Arrange the strips of cress round the edge of the salad.

3 To make the citrus dressing, put all the ingredients into a screwtop jar and shake well. Serve the salad with the citrus dressing.

This is an ideal salad for barbecues and al fresco eating and can be enjoyed on its own as a light snack or served as an accompaniment to other dishes.

melon
and prawn cocktail

4	Serves
15 minutes	Preparation time
10–12 minutes	Cooking time
225	Kcal
947	KJ
15 g	Protein
5 g	Fat
32 g	CHO

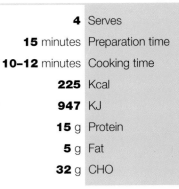

1 Bring a large saucepan of salted water to the boil. Add the pasta, stir and cook for 10–12 minutes until al dente. Rinse and drain well.

2 Mix the pasta, tomatoes, melon, prawns and cucumber together in a bowl. Make the dressing by mixing the mayonnaise, tomato ketchup, and yogurt and season with salt and pepper. Pour the dressing over the pasta mixture and toss well. To serve, spoon into glasses and sprinkle each with a little cayenne pepper.

125 g/4 oz spirali pasta

2 tomatoes, skinned and cut into
  8 pieces

½ honeydew melon, cubed

175 g/6 oz cooked peeled prawns

½ cucumber, cubed

½ teaspoon cayenne pepper

dressing:

3 tablespoons low-fat mayonnaise

1 tablespoon tomato ketchup

3 tablespoons low-fat natural
  yogurt

salt and pepper

Honeydew melons have smooth yellow skin and pale green or yellow flesh. Melon makes a very refreshing addition to this cocktail.

country salad

Serves	**4**
Preparation time	**15** minutes
Cooking time	about **12** minutes
Kcal	**276**
KJ	**1170**
Protein	**10** g
Fat	**5** g
CHO	**52** g

1 Bring a large saucepan of salted water to the boil. Add the pasta, stir and cook for 10–12 minutes until al dente. Drain well and mix with the olive oil, then leave to cool.

250 g/8 oz dried rigatoni pasta

2 teaspoons olive oil

4 tomatoes, skinned and chopped

1 green pepper, cored, deseeded and chopped

50 g/2 oz stuffed olives, sliced

175 g/6 oz button mushrooms, sliced

1 tablespoon tomato ketchup

6 tablespoons very low-fat yogurt

2 tablespoons lemon juice

salt and pepper

2 Mix the tomatoes, green pepper, olives and mushrooms into the pasta and season with salt and pepper. Mix the tomato ketchup with the yogurt and lemon juice, and stir into the salad until evenly coated.

Serve this salad on a bed of lettuce leaves. Curly endive or oak-leaf lettuce would be ideal.

coleslaw

4	Serves
10 minutes	Preparation time
73	Kcal
306	KJ
5 g	Protein
1 g	Fat
13 g	CHO

**500 g/1 lb white cabbage,
shredded**

125 g/4 oz carrots, grated

1 onion, sliced

**Lemon Yogurt Dressing
(see right)**

**1 tablespoon finely chopped
parsley, to garnish**

lemon yogurt dressing:

150 g/5 oz low-fat natural yogurt

1 tablespoon lemon juice

**2 teaspoons chopped mixed fresh
herbs**

salt and pepper

1 Mix the cabbage with the carrot and onion in a large bowl.

2 To make the lemon yogurt dressing, place all the ingredients in a bowl and whisk with a fork until well blended.

3 Add the lemon yogurt dressing and toss vigorously. Garnish with the chopped parsley and chill until ready to serve.

Coleslaw is very versatile and can be used as a garnish to main dishes, a filling for baked potatoes or as a side salad.

winter salad

Serves **6**

Preparation time **15** minutes

Cooking time about **12** minutes

Kcal **192**

KJ **809**

Protein **13** g

Fat **5** g

CHO **26** g

175 g/6 oz dried farfalle pasta

175 g/6 oz cooked, skinless
    chicken, diced

2 celery sticks, diced

2 red dessert apples, cored and
    diced

1 green pepper, cored, deseeded
    and diced

4 tablespoons low-fat mayonnaise

salt and pepper

½ lettuce head, to serve

1 Bring a large saucepan of salted water to the boil. Add the pasta, stir and cook for 10–12 minutes until al dente. Drain well and leave to cool.

2 Mix the chicken with the celery, apples, green pepper and pasta bows and season to taste with salt and pepper. Fold in the mayonnaise, turn into a salad bowl and serve with the lettuce, some of which could be shredded, if you like.

Use crisp red dessert apples, such as Braeburn, Empire or Jonathan, for this salad.

provençal
pasta salad

6	Serves
10–12 minutes	Preparation time
12 minutes	Cooking time
198	Kcal
839	KJ
14 g	Protein
5 g	Fat
26 g	CHO

175 g/6 oz dried rigatoni pasta

4 tablespoons low-fat mayonnaise

juice of ½ lemon

6 tomatoes, skinned, deseeded and
   chopped

125 g/4 oz French beans, cooked

12 black olives, pitted

200 g/7 oz can tuna in brine,
   drained and flaked

salt and pepper

1 small lettuce, shredded, to serve

50 g/2 oz can anchovy fillets,
   drained and washed, to garnish

1 Bring a large saucepan of salted water to the boil. Add the pasta, stir and cook for 10–12 minutes until al dente. Drain the pasta well. Mix the mayonnaise and lemon juice together and mix a little of this dressing with the pasta. Stir well to combine.

2 When the pasta is cool, turn into a bowl and mix with the tomatoes, beans, olives and tuna. Season with salt and pepper.

3 Toss the salad lightly in the remaining dressing and serve on a bed of shredded lettuce, garnished with anchovies.

Use vine-ripened tomatoes in this salad for a really full, sweet flavour.

courgette
and pasta salad

Serves	**4**
Preparation time	**10** minutes
Cooking time	**10–12** minutes
Kcal	**213**
KJ	**900**
Protein	**7** g
Fat	**5** g
CHO	**37** g

175 g/6 oz dried conchiglie pasta

3 tablespoons low-fat mayonnaise
diluted with 1 tablespoon tomato
juice

4 courgettes, sliced

2 tomatoes, skinned and chopped

8 pitted black olives

2 spring onions, chopped

1 tablespoon chopped parsley

salt and pepper

1 Bring a large saucepan of salted water to the boil. Add the pasta, stir and cook for 10–12 minutes until al dente. Rinse and drain well. While still warm, mix the pasta with the mayonnaise dressing.

2 Meanwhile, cook the courgettes in boiling salted water for 8 minutes until just tender, then drain and cool. Add to the pasta with the tomatoes, olives, spring onions and parsley and season with salt and pepper. Mix well and serve cold.

To prepare the spring onions, cut off the roots and most of the dark green leaves, then slice the remaining onion finely.

penne primavera

4	Serves
20 minutes	Preparation time
10 minutes	Cooking time
476	Kcal
2021	KJ
18 g	Protein
5 g	Fat
96 g	CHO

vinaigrette:

3 teaspoons olive oil

2 tablespoons cider or wine vinegar

2 teaspoons French mustard or

  1 teaspoon English mustard

1 teaspoon caster sugar

freshly grated nutmeg

1 garlic clove, crushed

salt and pepper

125 g/4 oz broccoli, broken into

  small pieces

125 g/4 oz French beans, cut into

  5 cm/2 inch lengths

125 g/4 oz mangetout

2 tablespoons chopped herbs

500 g/1 lb dried penne pasta

1 Steam the vegetables for 2–4 minutes until slightly softened but still brightly coloured and crisp. Drain, and put into a large bowl.

2 To make the vinaigrette, blend together all the ingredients and pour over the vegetables. Sprinkle the vegetables with the herbs.

3 Meanwhile, bring a large saucepan of salted water to the boil. Add the pasta, stir and cook for 10–12 minutes until al dente. Drain, and mix into the bowl of vegetables and vinaigrette. Serve either hot or cold.

Other vegetables that would be delicious in Penne Primavera include fennel, mushrooms, fresh peas, cauliflower, asparagus and red pepper.

desserts

It is important to indulge oneself, even when on a low-fat diet. These desserts are surprisingly low in fat. Many are fruit based, bursting with tempting colours and juicy flavours.

cheese hearts

Serves	**4**
Preparation time	**30** minutes, plus chilling
Kcal	**94**
KJ	**396**
Protein	**11** g
Fat	**3** g
CHO	**5** g

250 g/8 oz low-fat cottage cheese, sieved

artificial sweetener, to taste

150 ml/¼ pint natural yogurt

2 egg whites

1 tablespoon brandy

to decorate:

tiny fresh vine leaves (if available)

small clusters of black grapes

1 Mix the cottage cheese with a little sweetener to taste (if you don't have a very sweet tooth, this may not be necessary). Blend in the yogurt.

2 Whisk the egg whites until stiff but not dry. Fold lightly but thoroughly into the cheese mixture, together with the brandy.

3 Line 4 small perforated heart-shaped moulds with clean muslin. Spoon the cheese mixture into the lined moulds and cover with another layer of muslin.

4 Place the moulds on a tray or baking sheet with a rim, and chill for 6–8 hours. The excess liquid should have drained away from the cheese, and the moulds should be firm enough to turn out.

5 Unmould the hearts and decorate with vine leaves and clusters of grapes.

These cheese hearts are delicious served with a fresh fruit purée or coulis made from strawberries or raspberries.

peach granita

4	Serves
20–25 minutes, plus freezing	Preparation time
5 minutes	Cooking time
70	Kcal
290	KJ
2 g	Protein
1 g	Fat
9 g	CHO

1 Nick the stalk end of each peach. Plunge into a bowl of boiling water for 30–45 seconds, then slide off the skins. Halve the fruit, removing the stones, and chop the flesh roughly.

2 Put the peach flesh into a pan with the white wine and orange juice. Simmer gently for 5 minutes.

375 g/12 oz fresh ripe peaches
150 ml/¼ pint dry white wine
150 ml/¼ pint fresh orange juice
2 egg whites

3 Blend the peaches and the liquid in a food processor or blender until smooth. Cool.

4 Pour into a shallow freezer container and freeze until the granita is slushy around the edges, then tip into a bowl and break up the ice crystals.

5 Whisk the egg whites until stiff but not dry. Fold lightly but thoroughly into the partly-frozen granita, return to the container and freeze until firm.

To remove the stones from the peaches, slice them in half around the stone, through the groove, and twist the two halves to separate. Lever the stone out with a knife.

french apple flan

Serves	**10**
Preparation time	**15** minutes, plus chilling
Cooking time	**35–40** minutes
Kcal	**211**
KJ	**889**
Protein	**3** g
Fat	**5** g
CHO	**41** g

1 kg/2 lb cooking apples, peeled,
   cored, thinly sliced and puréed

2 red-skinned dessert apples, thinly
   sliced

50 g/2 oz caster sugar

4 tablespoons apricot jam

2 tablespoons lemon juice

pâte sucrée:

150 g/5 oz plain flour

50 g/2 oz butter

50 g/2 oz caster sugar

1 egg and 1 egg white, beaten
   together

few drops vanilla essence

1 To make the pâte sucrée, sift the flour on to a cool work surface. Make a well in the centre and add the butter, sugar, egg and egg white and vanilla essence. Using the fingertips of one hand, work these ingredients together, then draw in the flour. Knead lightly until smooth, then cover and chill for 1 hour.

2 Roll out the pastry very thinly on a floured work surface and use to line a 25 cm/10 inch fluted flan ring. Fill the case generously with the apple purée, then arrange an overlapping layer of sliced apples on top. Sprinkle with the sugar. Bake in a preheated oven, 190°C (375°F), Gas Mark 5, for 35–40 minutes.

3 Meanwhile, heat the jam with the lemon juice, then strain and brush over the apples. Serve hot or cold.

There is no need to grease tins when cooking this type of pastry because of the high fat content of the dough. In some other recipes the tins may need to be greased.

summer pudding

4 Serves

30 minutes, plus chilling | Preparation time

3 minutes | Cooking time

150 Kcal

620 KJ

5 g Protein

1 g Fat

30 g CHO

250 g/8 oz red and white currants

125 g/4 oz blackcurrants

125 g/4 oz raspberries

125 g/4 oz loganberries

125 g/4 oz strawberries

125 g/4 oz cherries, blueberries or
cultivated blackberries

1 tablespoon clear honey

margarine, for greasing

8 x 1 cm/½ inch thick slices brown
bread, crusts removed

1 Place all the fruit in a large saucepan (it must not be aluminium or cast iron) with the honey and cook very gently for 2–3 minutes, just long enough to soften the fruit and allow the juices to run a little.

2 Line a lightly greased 1.2 litre/ 2 pint pudding basin with three-quarters of the bread, trimming the slices to fit, making certain that all the surfaces are completely covered and the base has an extra thick layer.

3 Spoon in all the fruit, reserving 2 tablespoons of the juice in case the bread is not completely coloured by the fruit when the pudding is turned out. Cover with the remaining bread. Lay a plate or saucepan lid that will fit inside the rim of the bowl on top and place a 1 kg/2 lb weight on top of the plate or lid. Chill for 10–12 hours.

4 Turn out and cut into wedges to serve.

This classic English pudding is made with a selection of summer soft fruits which you can vary as you choose. Use one of the softer, lighter types of brown bread for this recipe.

stuffed figs

Serves	**4**
Preparation time	**10–15** minutes
Kcal	**4**
KJ	**135**
Protein	**4** g
Fat	**5** g
CHO	**20** g

**12 ripe fresh figs, preferably purple
ones**

3 tablespoons ground almonds

125 g/4 oz fresh raspberries

1 tablespoon clear honey

**4 vine leaves, soaked in warm
water and dried, to serve
(optional)**

1 Snip off any excess stalk from
each fig. Make a criss-cross cut
down from the stalk end and
carefully ease the cut open.

2 Mix the ground almonds with
the fresh raspberries and honey.

3 Place a vine leaf, spread out
flat, on each serving plate.
Arrange 3 figs on top of each one
and fill with the raspberry and
almond purée.

Look for unblemished figs which just yield when
held in the hand. Fig skin is soft and edible.

spiced pears

4		Serves
20	minutes	Preparation time
about **16**	minutes	Cooking time
86		Kcal
360		KJ
1	g	Protein
0	g	Fat
22	g	CHO

4 large firm pears

½ lemon

16 cloves

½ cinnamon stick

300 ml/½ pint red wine

2 tablespoons redcurrant jelly

4 orange slices

4 small fresh bay leaves, to

   decorate

1 Peel the pears, leaving the stalks intact. Rub them all over with the lemon half to prevent discoloration.

2 Stud each pear with 4 cloves. Stand them upright in a pan and add the cinnamon stick, wine and sufficient water just to cover the pears.

3 Bring to the boil and simmer gently until the pears are just tender. Leave to cool in the cooking liquid.

4 Put 2 tablespoons of the cooking liquid into a small pan with the redcurrant jelly. Bubble briskly for about 1 minute until the jelly has dissolved.

5 Place an orange slice on each of 4 small plates. Drain the pears with a slotted spoon, and sit one on top of each orange slice.

6 Spoon a little of the redcurrant glaze over each pear and decorate with a bay leaf.

Use large, firm pears for this recipe; Anjou, Beurré Dumont, Conference or Williams would be ideal.

orange
diet cheesecake

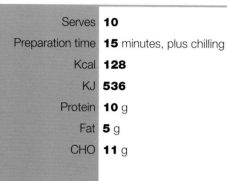

Serves	**10**
Preparation time	**15** minutes, plus chilling
Kcal	**128**
KJ	**536**
Protein	**10** g
Fat	**5** g
CHO	**11** g

40 g/1½ oz low-fat spread, softened

8 digestive biscuits, crushed

125 g/4 oz very low-fat cottage
 cheese

4 tablespoons skimmed milk

375 g/12 oz quark cheese

3 tablespoons orange juice

grated rind of 2 oranges

artificial liquid sweetener, to taste

2 eggs, separated

15 g/½ oz powdered gelatine

3 tablespoons water

4 large oranges

1 Lightly grease an 18 cm/7 inch loose-bottomed cake tin with a little of the low-fat spread. Mix the remaining spread with the biscuit crumbs. Spoon evenly over the base of the cake tin and press down firmly with the back of a wooden spoon.

2 Meanwhile, purée the cottage cheese and milk in a blender until smooth. Mix together the quark, cottage cheese mixture, orange juice, three-quarters of the rind and artificial sweetener to taste. Beat the egg yolks into the mixture, one at a time, beating well after each addition.

3 Sprinkle the gelatine over the water in a small heatproof bowl and leave for a few minutes until spongy. Place the bowl in a saucepan of hot water and stir over a very gentle heat until dissolved. Allow to cool slightly, then stir into the cheese mixture. Chill in the refrigerator until thick and just beginning to set. Whisk the egg whites stiffly, then fold them into the cheese mixture, using a large metal spoon.

4 Pour the cheese mixture over the crumb base. Smooth the surface and chill in the refrigerator for about 5 hours until set.

5 Peel and divide the oranges into segments. Decorate the top edge of the cheesecake with the larger, better-looking slices and sprinkle the centre with the remaining rind.

yogurt-fruit cup

6	Serves
10 minutes, plus chilling	Preparation time
124	Kcal
526	KJ
4 g	Protein
3 g	Fat
23 g	CHO

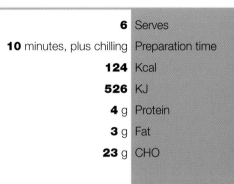

500 g/1 lb can sliced peaches
or sliced pears in fruit juice,
drained

475 ml/16 fl oz low-fat vanilla
yogurt

to decorate:

2 tablespoons finely chopped
toasted almonds

½ teaspoon ground cardamom, to
garnish

1 Divide the sliced peaches or sliced pears evenly among 6 small glass dessert bowls, in layers.

2 Top each bowl with an equal quantity of the yogurt and chill in the refrigerator until required.

3 To serve, sprinkle each bowl lightly with the toasted almonds and garnish with ground cardamom.

This recipe offers a new twist to a back-to-basics favourite. It is ideal for preparing in advance and you'll like the fragrant touch of cardamom. It would also make a refreshing breakfast alternative, by substituting the almonds with muesli.

melon ice cream

Serves	**4**
Preparation time	**20–25** minutes, plus freezing
Kcal	**90**
KJ	**380**
Protein	**5** g
Fat	**0** g
CHO	**16** g

1 large melon (Ogen or Charentais)

300 ml/½ pint natural yogurt

1 Halve the melon and scoop out all the seeds. Scoop the melon flesh into a food processor or blender and work until smooth.

2 Mix the melon purée with the yogurt.

3 Transfer the melon and yogurt mixture to a shallow freezer container, and freeze until firm.

4 Serve the melon ice cream in scoops.

To achieve the 2 different colours, use 2 different types of melon: Charentais melon for peachy-orange ice cream and Ogen for green.

strawberry ice

4 Serves

25 minutes, plus freezing | Preparation time

126 Kcal

525 KJ

7 g Protein

5 g Fat

14 g CHO

3 egg yolks

1 tablespoon redcurrant jelly

1 tablespoon red vermouth

300 ml/½ pint natural yogurt

375 g/12 oz ripe strawberries,
    hulled

4–6 strawberries, with stalks,
    halved, to decorate

1 Put the egg yolks into a blender or food processor with the redcurrant jelly, vermouth, yogurt and half the strawberries and blend until smooth.

2 Transfer the mixture to a shallow freezerproof container, and freeze until the ice cream starts to harden around the edges.

3 Tip the ice cream into a bowl and beat to break up the ice crystals.

4 Chop the remaining strawberries and mix them into the half-frozen ice cream. Return the ice cream to the container and freeze until quite firm.

5 Scoop the ice cream into stemmed glasses and decorate each one with strawberry halves.

Yogurt adds a piquant flavour to ice cream. Eat the ice cream soon after it is frozen before it becomes too hard.

Index

Acknowledgements

Octopus Publishing Group Ltd./Martin Brigdale 83, 88. /Philip Dowell 26, 138. /David Loftus 7, 8, 9, 10. /Diana Miller 14, 15, 16, 17, 18, 19, 20, 21, 23, 24, 25. /Hilary Moore 12-13, 22, 43, 49, 51, 58, 64, 73, 103, 112, 130-131, 134, 140. /Vernon Morgan 50, 62, 132, 136, 137. /James Murphy 78, 110, 117. /Simon Smith 5, 6, 27, 28, 29, 30, 31, 32, 33, 34, 36, 37, 38, 40-41, 44, 47, 48, 54, 55, 56, 57, 59, 60-61, 66, 68, 71, 74, 75, 76-77, 79, 80, 81, 82, 84, 85, 86, 87, 89, 90, 91, 92, 93, 94, 95, 96, 98, 99, 100, 101, 102, 104, 106-107, 108, 109, 113, 114, 115, 118, 120, 121, 123, 124, 126, 127, 128, 129. /Clive Streeter 42, 53, 67. /Trevor Wood 69